GANONG
A Sweet History of Chocolate

GANONG

A Sweet History of Chocolate

DAVID FOLSTER

Cover photograph: Roger Smith.
Cover and interior design by Julie Scriver.
Printed in Canada.
10 9 8 7 6 5 4 3 2 1

Library and Archives Canada Cataloguing in Publication

Folster, David
Ganong: a sweet history of chocolate / David Folster.

Includes index.
ISBN 0-86492-480-1

1. Ganong Bros. Ltd. — History. 2. Candy industry — New Brunswick —
St. Stephen — History. I. Title.

HD9330.C654G36 2006   338.7'6641530971533   C2006-904727-8

Goose Lane Editions acknowledges the financial support of the Canada Council for the Arts,
the Government of Canada through the Book Publishing Industry Development Program (BPIDP),
and the New Brunswick Department of Wellness, Culture and Sport for its publishing activities.

Goose Lane Editions
Suite 330, 500 Beaverbrook Court
Fredericton, New Brunswick
CANADA E3B 5X4
www.gooselane.com

CONTENTS

AUTHOR'S NOTE

A book like this can't be created without the help of others. In particular, I want to thank Cheryl Hewitt, who, in addition to her other duties with Ganong, serves as company archivist and does the job with great diligence and passion. Others who helped with their insights into the company history and corporate ethos were Greg Fash, Jim Eagles, and David Hawkins. Dianne Lombard of St. Stephen's Chocolate Museum, Jeff McShane of the Ganong Chocolatier, and Pat Orr of Ganong were helpful in my contacts with them, as was Dr. W.F. Ganong's daughter, Ann Seidler, of New York. Valuable assistance came, too, from Marion Beyea, Fred Farrell, Wanda Lyons, and Rob Gilmore of the Provincial Archives of New Brunswick; Jean Weissenhorn DeLong and Kathleen Jeffries of the New Brunswick Legislative Library; Daryl Johnson and Stephen Clayden of the New Brunswick Museum; Pat Belier and Patti Auld Johnson of the Harriet Irving Library at the University of New Brunswick; and Rhonda Baker Gordon of NB Power. A special thanks to Doug Dougherty of the Charlotte County Museum, who, on a chilling January day, pored over old photographs with me in the museum, which was closed for the winter. Thanks, also, to Judy Hiscock of Skyline Transcription Services, Art MacKay of the St. Croix Estuary Project, and Susan Fussell of the (U.S.) National Confectioners Association. And, finally, my appreciation to the people at Goose Lane Editions, who assigned Rebecca Leaman to edit the book and Julie Scriver to design it; the skills they brought to the task are, I think, self-evident.

— *David Folster*

Water Street
St. Stephen, N.B.

St. Stephen's main street near the turn of the century. Charlotte County Museum

INTRODUCTION

In 1873, at the beginning of a great transitional period in North American society, a Canadian chocolate company was born in the most unlikely of places. The company was Ganong Brothers, and the place was the small town of St. Stephen, New Brunswick, on the St. Croix River, just across from Calais, Maine.

Today that company has the distinction of being the oldest family-owned candy business in Canada. It still has a Ganong at its helm, and, in inspired defiance of the fate that has often befallen businesses in the country's easternmost provinces, it is still in St. Stephen, still going strong, even in the age of conglomerates and globalization.

Because the company was founded about the same time as many of the other famous names in the confectionery business, the Ganong story is really the history of chocolate- and candy-making in North America. The year the two Ganong brothers started out in business, Canada itself was a mere six years old, and in the ensuing decades the company faced the usual crises of a fledgling enterprise in a newborn nation — fires, economic depressions, huge changes in business and society — and overcame them all. One thing that surely helped near the beginning was Sir John A. Macdonald's National Policy of 1878, which protected homegrown industries by raising tariffs on imported goods and lowering customs duties on raw materials. Ganong turned out to be an exception — one of the few National Policy industries that survive to this day.

The two brothers who started the company, James and Gilbert Ganong, didn't intend to be candy-makers. Raised at the head of Belleisle Bay, in southern New

Brunswick's beautiful St. John River country, they might have followed their father into his occupations of farming and operating a general store. But James, for one, loved horses and wanted to be a jockey, and after honing his skills in races on the mud flats of Courtenay Bay, near Saint John, he moved to Boston and more racing. This lasted until growing family responsibilities, and a few extra pounds he'd put on, forced him to quit jockeying and take a job as a salesman for a biscuit company. His brother Gilbert, meanwhile, had gone into teaching and was on a path that he hoped would lead to becoming a medical doctor.

Instead, the two wound up as business partners in a mill and shipbuilding town hard by the American border, first as grocers and, presently, as makers of candy. And so began a saga that is a reflection of Canada itself as it grew into a mature nation, a social history that is built around a romantic product and peopled with remarkable characters.

One of the cornerstones of the company's longevity has been the determination of the Ganong family, now in its fifth generation at the business, to stay right in the town where the venture began — to stay there even in the face of nearly irresistible offers that frequently came in from rivals, who would have delighted at removing such an estimable competitor from the marketplace fray. As far as the Ganongs were concerned, acceptance of any of those offers ultimately would have doomed the company in St. Stephen, a repeat of the traditional Maritime experience with absentee ownership. So the offers were always politely refused, and life went on.

The town benefited and so did the company and out of this relationship emerged an enterprise that became a part of our national lore and one of the most prolific candy companies in North America, one that at times produced as many as eleven hundred different kinds of chocolates and confections. The company's creations include the world's first five-cent chocolate nut bar, the All-Day Sucker, and that wonderfully unique Maritime Christmas candy, the Chicken

Bone. Ganong was also one of the first Canadian companies to sell boxed chocolates, and one of its brands, Delecto, has been familiar to chocolate fanciers for nearly one hundred years. Another famous incarnation came in the 1930s, when Ganong Brothers eased Great Depression blues with its heart-shaped Valentine boxes, and a new symbol of Canadian romance was born.

"All gone and ready for more. That's the way I feel about them."

Ganong's GB Chocolates

These wares had to be promoted, of course, and company advertisements, like the colour posters displayed on Canadian streetcars early in the last century, and the full-page advertisements in *Maclean's* in the 1930s, represent milestones of their own. These advertising materials and the vintage Ganong chocolate boxes, all carefully preserved in the company's archives and at St. Stephen's Chocolate Museum, are at the heart of this illustrated history. They mirror Canada's dramatic transformation from an agrarian to a manufacturing nation and the beginning of the age of consumerism. They also provide a sense of why the company has survived all these years.

Not that it's been easy. Several times Ganong has gone to the brink, then come to its own rescue. It happened again in the 1990s, and forced the company, now under fourth-generation president David Ganong, in effect to re-invent itself. There's a temptation to say that ultimately what this proves is that life is sweet, and small is beautiful. But there have been times when the Ganong story was bittersweet at best. And, meanwhile, this company must grow, too, just like its rivals, to survive in a business dominated by huge competitors. How Ganong is managing that in the twenty-first century is the story of a unique alchemy born of creative leadership and long-held principles, and one that's good for the Canadian soul.

St. Stephen and Calais waterfronts in the days of sail. Charlotte County Museum

J. H. GANONG.

G. W. GANONG.

Office of GANONG BROS.,

Manufacturing Confectioners, Bakers,

DEALERS IN

Foreign and Domestic Fruits, Nuts, Canned Goods, &c.

ST. STEPHEN, N. B.

Our Mr *J H Ganong* will be at your place on or about *Dec 16th*

STARTING OUT
From the Brink to a Business

The announcement in the weekly *Saint Croix Courier* of St. Stephen, New Brunswick, on June 5, 1873, bore no hint of what might follow. All it said was,

> Mr. G.W. Ganong has opened a store in the premises lately
> occupied by Mr. A.H. Clewley, in the Courier Building, where
> he intends to keep on hand a stock of fresh fruit, vegetables and
> country produce. He makes a specialty of Thurston Hall & Cos
> crackers, which embrace almost every variety and are done up
> in tin cases of convenient size for family use. The rate at which
> they are sold is very reasonable, and being put up in air tight cans
> they are all well preserved. Many a worthy housewife may save
> much trouble and fatigue in the matter of baking by patronizing
> Mr. Ganong.

Nobody, not even G.W. Ganong himself, could have imagined that this was actually the beginning of what would be, more than a century and a quarter later, a Canadian confectionery business that would be as rich in tradition and romance as some of its own candy pieces.

All that G.W. (Gilbert) and his brother James intended was to become grocers serving customers in the vicinity of the St. Croix River. It was James's idea. Working as a salesman, or drummer, for the Thurston & Hall Biscuit Company of

James Harvey Ganong.

Cambridgeport, Massachusetts, he yearned to start his own business. He thought St. Stephen would be a good place because its border location would allow him to keep his job with the biscuit company while he nurtured the new business into existence. Needing a partner, and one with a little nest-egg at that, he talked Gilbert, who was then teaching and saving his money for medical school, into joining him.

The venture was soon in trouble. It turned out that St. Stephen and the nearby worker community of Milltown were already well supplied with grocers, and local housewives didn't seem much interested in patronizing two strangers in town whom scarcely anybody knew. If Gilbert, who took charge of the store while James continued drumming for the biscuit company, hadn't discovered a trade in certain specialty items, the business almost certainly would have failed.

The items were fruit, nuts, oysters from Chesapeake Bay, and, most fortuitously, candy. Even so, the brothers were still in for a tough battle, for St. Stephen already had a competent confectioner, a man named Charles Holt. Once Holt learned the Ganongs were trying to compete with him, he moved quickly to upstage them. He opened a well-appointed new store and lavishly displayed his candies in its windows. Consequently, by Christmas, 1873, the Ganong enterprise was again teetering on the brink.

On New Year's Day, 1874, Gilbert sat at a desk and began a practice that he would continue each January 1st for the next several years. He composed an annual diary entry in which he recorded the events of the previous twelve months in business and set out his plans and hopes for the next twelve. The diary has survived, and it provides both a detailed account of those early, difficult days and rare insights into the character of an intensely private man who was then in the process of establishing what would prove to be one of the most durable of Canadian businesses.

As Gilbert recorded, their competitor Holt attacked fiercely in early 1874, cutting his prices to wholesale customers in a bid to finish off the Ganongs. The effort backfired, however, because many of those customers were irritated that Holt hadn't offered better prices earlier, and they switched to the Ganongs as suppliers. With his business declining, Holt now found himself overextended as a result of his borrowing to outfit the new store, and presently he was at Gilbert's door offering to sell the rest of his wholesale trade and to rent himself out to the Ganongs as a baker and candy-maker. They declined, full in the knowledge that they had won the first competitive battle of their young careers.

Meanwhile, there were other problems to deal with. They had great trouble finding a suitable clerk for the store so that Gilbert could make sales trips into the countryside. Several prospects revealed a propensity for drink, a condition for which Gilbert, an absolute teetotaler, had little tolerance. There was also a problem with pilferage. Then, in 1875, the effects of a world-wide depression, triggered by a banking collapse in the United States, descended on the St. Croix valley. As it took hold of the local economy, Gilbert christened 1875 "the Year of Failures."

Through all this, however, he retained a remarkable equanimity, and for a not unusual reason: he was in love. Her name was Maria Robinson, and she was the attractive, well-bred daughter of a prominent local merchant. The romance did wonders for Gilbert's spirits. "With this feeling," he confided to his diary on January 1, 1876, "I enter another year with renewed hopes and, I trust, higher aspirations."

They were married that October. By then, the business had again righted itself and was at last showing true signs of growth. With two local candy-makers in their employ, the Ganongs began selling in Saint John, and before the year was out they reached into Nova Scotia. "One more year with as good business as last," wrote Gilbert at New Year's, 1877, "I think will put us in position to feel perfectly safe." Four and a half months later, their small factory was in ruins. A terrible fire that started in the hayloft of their horse barn swept through St. Stephen and destroyed

Gilbert White Ganong.

much of the downtown. Gilbert and friends managed to save some stock and fixtures and a few personal items, but it was still a devastating loss. However, the brothers rallied quickly, reassured their creditors, and found temporary quarters until a new building was ready a couple of months later. Resiliency, it seems, was already a Ganong hallmark.

During the past year I have been decidedly blest. I may have lost some professed friends and tried the ties of others, in doing what, after much careful deliberation, I believed to be my right and duty. If I have lost the confidence of some, I am more than repaid by the better knowledge and closer ties of others in whom my hopes centre and whose friendship has shown no wavering, and in whose more intimate association I expect to enjoy my future years. With this feeling, I enter another year with renewed hopes and, I trust, higher aspirations.

— Gilbert Ganong diary entry,
January 1, 1876

fearful Leakage last year. For where
our profits have only been $800 more
than estimated profits on last years
sales, our Losses have been 600
more, and we have made about
$900 more money, showing a Deficit
of from 900 to 1000 in 1874. It makes
a fellow feel as if there might be
something better yet to come, if we
are only fitted to work it out.
We are not likely to lose more
than 1/2 the amt. of Debts next
year we have lost this, and will
probably handle 5000 more mdse.
During the Past year I have been
Socially blest. I may have lost some
Professed Friends and tried the ties
of others, in doing what after much
careful deliberation I believed to be
my Right and duty. If I have
lost the confidence of some I am
more than repaid by the better
knowledge and closer ties of others

in whom my hopes centre and
whose friendship has shown no
wavering, and in whose more intimate association I expect to enjoy
my future years. With this belief
I enter another year with renewed
hopes and I trust higher aspirations.

Statistics

	Sold	Cash Sales		Sold	cus.
Jan.	5.12	263.67			
Feb.	24.48	280.20	July	65.69	479.00
Mar.	22.85	393.27	Aug.	50.18	426.58
Apl.	29.15	842.91	Sept.	54.30	500.45
May	28.70	506.82	Oct.	41.17	491.62
June	98.20	511.65	Nov.	36.63	393.44
			Dec.	42.15	537.38
Total					483.54

N.S. $5-26.49

Cash Receipts for year.. $5-610.03

Losses by absconding Debtors $

among other Failures were   Jno. Brown   35.01

Vaughan, A. B. Coombs   J. M. Epps.   90.00

A. Olliver, J. C. Murray   E. S. Norcross   206.74

Stewart & Woodcock.   J. C. Rogers   41.06

Roberts & Ross $372.81

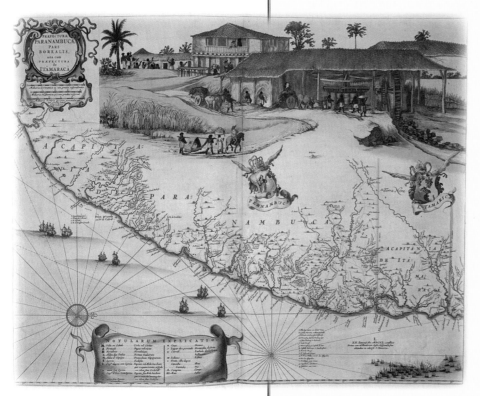

Sugar Works and Plantation,
Pernambuco, Brazil, c. 1640.

Joan Blaeu, *Atlas maior, sive Graographia Balvinia* (Amsterdam,
circa 1662), Special Collections Department, University of Virginia

People have been making candy for at least four thousand years. It started with apothecaries and healers who, although they coated seeds, nuts, herbs, beans, and fruits with honey merely to help the medicine go down, sometimes created rather tasty morsels that their patients kept eating long after they'd been cured.

Sugar, of course, was the ingredient that transformed candy-making — in fact, the very word "candy" derived from the Persian word for sugar, *kansifed*. From India and the valley of the Nile, sugarcane spread through the world's warmer climes, and as it did, and as sugar became more widely available, people began creating imaginative confections. The French, for example, developed nougat and the praline and, later on, various pieces of candy-making apparatus. The English specialized in "boiled sweets," which they trotted out in great abundance for London's Great Exhibition of

All Nations in 1851, from where they soon reached the rest of Europe and North America, too.

On this side of the Atlantic, the availability of sugar depended on where you lived. The feminist Nellie McClung remembered her mother making "vinegar pies" because there wasn't much sugar on the Manitoba prairie late in the nineteenth century. It was also relatively unknown in other parts of Canada, although a worthy substitute was maple syrup, which an early traveler to northern New Brunswick found "very delicious . . . wholesome and even medicinal."

Sugar was more available closer to the coast, and regular shipments of raw sugar from the West Indies transformed East Coast ports like Philadelphia, Baltimore, and Newport, Massachusetts, into candy-making centres. St. Stephen, situated on the estuary of the St. Croix River, was a port, too, and schooners carrying lumber from St. Croix sawmills down to the West Indies loaded up their holds for the return trip with rum, sugar, and molasses. The teetotaling Ganongs didn't do anything with the rum. But they certainly made the most of the sugar and molasses.

A sugar vendor, circa 1700.
Toronto Reference Library

Ganong's barley sticks were an early stock item in the world of confectionery.

James Edwin Ganong.

In 1878, only a year after the big fire, James and Gilbert Ganong joined an American partner named James Picard in starting a soap works in St. Stephen. Considering that their candy business was still very much a fledgling, this might have seemed a remarkably bold, even foolhardy, thing to do. But this was the last quarter of the nineteenth century, and the entrepreneurial spirit was everywhere rampant. Canada was turning the corner toward becoming a manufacturing nation, and the following year Sir John A. Macdonald's National Policy, which raised the tariff on imported goods and lowered duties on incoming raw materials, boosted this trend further.

Besides, the Ganong brothers had already proved themselves adept at business. As their hometown newspaper editorialized, they were succeeding in the candy business by making an excellent product, "and the same course pursued in this new branch of manufacture cannot fail to produce like results."

The St. Croix Soap Manufacturing Company did succeed, so well, in fact, that within half a dozen years of its start-up, James and Gilbert agreed to dissolve their partnership. Gilbert remained in charge of the candy factory, while James gave himself over to full-time management of the soap works.

Inside, the St. Croix plant on Depot Street looked like something that might have been spawned by the midnight musings of a mad scientist. But from this mélange of vats and cauldrons and vaporous columns came some fifty tons of various soaps every week. They included a floating bath soap called Sea Foam and a soap powder named White Cross. By far the most popular and best known, however, was an ochre-coloured cake soap that was called Surprise because it cleaned "the surprise way, without boiling or scalding." Housewives testified to its versatility and effectiveness, and in Maritime homes Surprise Soap became almost as indispensable as the pail and the mop.

James Ganong was still running the company when, in the damp spring of 1888, he came down with a cold. At first, it seemed like nothing a few days of rest couldn't cure. But then it progressed into pneumonia. The family sent for two of his children who were away at school. Neither made it home in time. He died on April 21, at age forty-seven. A huge funeral followed as St. Stephen mourned a man the local newspaper called "one of its best citizens."

After James's death, his son Edwin took over the soap works. He, too, was a go-getter, and the company continued to flourish, eventually requiring four additions. Ed ran the business until the First World War, when it was sold to Lever Brothers. He moved to Toronto as a Lever executive, and the St. Stephen plant kept operating through the end of the Second World War. But Ed died in 1944, and three years later the St. Croix plant was shut down permanently, making it part of a burdensome legacy that has always haunted Maritime towns. As a newspaper in Saint John said, it was "just one of dozens of examples of what happens when control of our local industries passes outside the province."

St. Croix Soap Manufacturing Company, St. Stephen, N.B.
Provincial Archives of New Brunswick, P128-144

Surprise Soap customers could redeem coupons for valuable gifts listed in the company's catalogue.

A TEXTILE MILL ON THE ST. CROIX

The move to the St. Croix Soap Manufacturing Company hardly quieted James Ganong's restless boosterism. Soon, he was involved in another venture, this one to build a textile mill on the border. The idea was to duplicate on the St. Croix what had been done in many New England river towns. A site was chosen in the worker community of Milltown, New Brunswick, just upriver from St. Stephen.

Planning proceeded well enough at first, but then a kind of ennui crept in, and the project might have collapsed entirely if it hadn't been for James Ganong. At a critical meeting of local businessmen in a Calais office one waning March afternoon, he grew increasingly frustrated with the long, tedious, and seemingly endless discussion. Finally leaping to his feet, he walked to the door, locked it, and then told those assembled that they couldn't leave until they came to a decision. The businessmen pulled themselves together, pledged some money, and built the cotton mill that became Milltown's mainstay for seventy years.

COTTON MILL. DEMOLISHED ABOUT 1969.

The cotton mill at Milltown.
Charlotte County Museum

23

Above left: the Ganong factory, early 1900s; the company store is on the right.

THE CANDY-MAKERS

As their business grew, the Ganong brothers began to sense its inherent possibilities. Perhaps they could build a company whose products would sell far beyond St. Stephen's borders, maybe even throughout the whole country. But they also realized that, for that to happen, they would have to find better candy-making talent than was available locally.

Canada, in only its second full decade of existence, was still a largely frontier place. It had little in the way of a candy-making tradition. In the Ganongs' home province of New Brunswick, for example, about the only time early settlers tasted candy was at Christmas, when an ambitious housewife might, if the ingredients happened to be available, whip up a batch of walnut toffee using a recipe brought from the Old Country. Even in the civilized little provincial capital of Fredericton, candy was still so rare that, when a confectioner opened a shop in 1867, a local newspaper praised him for at last freeing the citizenry from the bondage of cheap, imported goods and praised his "Sweets of Life" as a sign of the town's "progressive mood."

In St. Stephen, the Ganong brothers, having decided to concentrate on confectionery, at first employed ordinary bakers to make it for them, including, at last, their erstwhile competitor, Charles Holt, until the poor fellow's sudden death. Bakers, naturally, were more accustomed to making bread and the mariners' hard biscuit known as pilot. So, as the Gilded Age wore on, and people's tastes evolved, Gilbert realized he needed people who'd actually been schooled in the subtle science of candy-making if he hoped to sell farther afield.

A group of Ganong candy-makers, 1880s.

As it happened, he got the first of these purely by luck. One day, sometime in the mid-1880s, a young man showed up at his office and asked for a job. His name was Christian Laubman, and he came from Germany, where his family had been confectioners for generations. Gilbert hired him on the spot and set him to work making lozenges, his family's specialty. Chris Laubman, who would stay with Ganong's for the rest of his life, gave the company an early pre-eminence in lozenges, and, equally important, ushered in the era of the trained professional candy-maker at Ganong's.

These men — four others joined Laubman over a fifteen-year period — were true artisans who would constitute as good a cadre of candy-making expertise as existed in North America. All would have long careers at Ganong's, and even well after they were gone, the walls of the old factory still echoed tales of how they had created this or that distinctive candy piece and of what rare characters they all had been.

The first to arrive after Laubman was Frank Sparhawk, a little fellow with a moustache. Gilbert found him in the American candy-making centre of Baltimore, Maryland. Sparhawk was a hard-candy specialist with a reputation for being able to "pull" five hundred and fifty pounds of stick candy every day. Nobody at the St. Stephen factory believed it — until they watched him do it. Sadly, Sparhawk wasn't able to make his wife a believer in St. Stephen itself, and she left with their son after just three months, never to return. But the little candy-maker stayed put. His creations for Ganong's would include stick candy, a penny favourite of youngsters, who loved the little figures and messages he magically embedded in the centres of the sticks, and the Chicken Bone, an item that would become a Maritime Christmas tradition.

After Sparhawk came George F. Ensor, in answer to Gilbert's advertisement in the Baltimore newspapers for a "gum-and-jelly" man. He said he'd stay for two weeks, long enough to teach the locals how to make good gumdrops. But when he sailed up the St. Croix and saw St. Stephen mouldering at low tide, his reaction was like that of Mrs. Sparhawk, only with a shorter fuse. Seeing the decaying wharves and the masted schooners perched high and dry, seemingly left on the beaches to rot, he was hell-bent for catching the next boat back to Baltimore. But then the tide came in, and the place suddenly looked a whole lot better. Ensor decided to stay and, except for vacations, never left. Called the Scholar because he always wore a suit and had a pince-nez perched on his nose, he was with Ganong's for forty years. He became one of North America's outstanding candy-makers, expert not only at making gums and jellies but also at mixing chocolate and delicately shaded cream candies. He was also Gilbert's alter ego, a stickler for standards and precision, and the Ganongs would always credit George Ensor as the single individual most responsible for the reputation their company gained for quality and excellence.

One more former Baltimore candy-maker who found his niche in St. Stephen was Edward Bosein. A specialist in "pan" work (named for a French invention, the revolving pan), Bosein was a dark and brooding loner who also had the ability to get under the Ganongs' skin occasionally. One time was during the First World War, when he put a map of Europe on a factory wall and began plotting enemy advances on it, apparently in deference to his German heritage and despite having a son serving with the Canadian forces. Only the intervention of Arthur Ganong, Gilbert's nephew, who was by then running the business and ordered the map taken down, prevented a mini-outbreak of hostilities within the factory.

George F. Ensor, candy-maker and factory superintendent, 1889 to 1929.

But while Bosein's national allegiances could be questioned — more likely, he was simply being ornery and stubborn — no one ever doubted his versatility at making candy. Over the years, he invented many pieces, including one not long after the map brouhaha was resolved. Asked in 1919 to create a chocolate bar that had the texture of a piece of cheese, he came up with a centre of yellow fudge and coconut coated with chocolate and peanuts. The new bar which the company called Pal-o-Mine, invoked such a sense of loyalty that today it is one of the oldest continuously produced candy bars in North America.

The last candy-maker to join Ganong's in that critical fifteen years of the company's development was a doughty Scottish "sugar-boiler" named Alex Reid. Reid was a caramel expert, and he could make them just about every way imaginable — hard or soft, quick-melting or slow, for dipping in chocolate or ready for wrapping. Presiding over his cauldrons, he had the rare ability to be able to tell, just from the way the bubbles burst, when a batch was ready for pouring onto the steel cooling tables. He

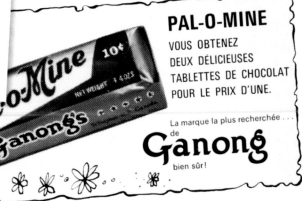

Packing Pal-o-Mine bars, 1942.

Tools of the early candy-maker's trade: a "hand depositor" used in making lozenges; a candy roller, hard candy cutter, viscometer, and a lozenge cutter.

never missed, and Alex Reid's many variations on the theme of caramel became important staples of the Ganong business.

Other candy-makers came along in the ensuing decades, including some very good homegrown ones, and they helped make Ganong's one of the most prolific confectioners in North America. By the 1930s, the company was producing, at any given moment, nearly eleven hundred different candies. But it was the quintet of Laubman, Sparhawk, Ensor, Bosein, and Reid who provided the foundation and made it possible for this Maritime company to come to national prominence just as Canadians were finding the time and money for a sweet new indulgence.

REVOLVING PAN WITHOUT THE HEATING COILS

Style "A" Handle

Style "B" Handle

WHERE CHOCOLATE CAME FROM
AND HOW IT GOT HERE

 It took chocolate a long time to become the tasty treat it is today. Its roots lay literally in the rich organic soils of the Central and South American rainforests, where the broad-leafed cacao tree grew more than four thousand years ago. In the ripe, golden pods that hung from the tree's trunk, native people found beans with which they made a powerful drink. The Aztecs of Mexico called the drink *chocolatl*. Emperor Montezuma II used it for fabulous feasts — and for (possibly) fabulous feats: before entering his harem, he always fortified himself with *chocolatl* drunk from a new golden goblet, which he then tossed in a lake; there were a lot of golden goblets in that lake.

Among the people who took the beans to Europe was Christopher Columbus. But it was the Spanish conquistador Hernán Cortés who told his fellow countrymen that the beans should be used to make "the divine drink . . . which builds up resistance and fights fatigue." After that, chocolate traveled Europe with the same all-encompassing reputation as a patent medicine: it was an aphrodisiac (the Montezuma theory, shared by many others), a stomach settler (as Samuel Pepys wrote in his *Diaries*), or as a cure for maladies such as syphilis. No wonder that, in a cosmopolitan place like London, "chocolate houses" came to rival the city's legendary coffee houses, or that their chief customers were those sporty young gents the English called "bloods."

Over in Holland, however, a patient Dutchman pursued a higher purpose for chocolate. In the early 1800s, after a long series of experiments, Coenraad Johannes van Houten invented the machine known as the cocoa press. Through a process of pressing and filtering, van Houten was able to extract a rich "butter" from the ground beans and create soluble cocoa. It was then found that, by adding the cocoa butter and sugar to the residual paste or "liquor" of the ground beans, one could make moulded bars of edible chocolate. With that discovery, this ancient Mayan and Aztec foodstuff was ready for conversion to confectionery, and the candy business changed forever.

Photos ©Zajcskowski, Lagui, Dreamstime.com

Moulds for chocolate Easter items, scale calibration weights, candy thermometer.

CHOCOLATES *and* PENNY CANDIES

In the early 1890s, another depression hit, sending businesses everywhere into a tailspin. Naturally, confectionery businesses, of which there were now many more, were affected, too. But at Ganong Brothers — the firm had kept its original name even after James moved to the soap works — Gilbert Ganong made a decision that would shape the company for all time: he decided it should become known as a chocolate company.

With the dawning of the era of conspicuous consumption, the candy trade had become highly competitive, and the arrival of another depression simply made it more so. Even staples of the business — gumdrops, jelly beans, lozenges, coconut pieces, and the like — became a hard sell. So Gilbert decided that his company should push its better lines of chocolates.

It was a smart decision. Barely a decade and a half earlier, when he and James were just starting out, chocolate had been virtually a negligible commodity in North America; within a few years, it would become the rage of the confectionery business. In 1901, the value

36

of imported cocoa and its products reached half a million dollars, and the amount would nearly double over the next four years.

At Ganong's, all the best chocolates were stamped with the letters G.B., which stood not so much for the company name as for Gilbert's promise that these were "Ganong's Best." It was a process of which he was both proud and protective, accomplished by placing each freshly hand-dipped chocolate on a celluloid pad embossed with the letters. He first patented the process and then took the unusual step of warning his competitors not to infringe on the patent. He also gave salesmen a bonus for selling G.B. Chocolates, and those sales, as a result, shot up.

So, in the midst of a depression, Ganong Brothers actually prospered. In this, the company contrasted starkly with other Maritime industries that the National Policy, with its protective tariffs, had stimulated into existence. Discouraged by periodic recessions and other debilitating factors, such as geographical disadvantage, high freight rates, and the heavier political clout of central Canada, many gave up the battle and either failed or capitulated to outside interests. The Milltown cotton mill passed quietly to a Montreal-controlled combine in 1892, and three formerly independent sugar refineries were amalgamated into one, owned by Scottish interests, in 1894.

Part of the reason Ganong Brothers flourished was that, despite the depression early in the decade, the candy business eventually soared in the Gay Nineties. It went from being a North American industry worth no more than two or three million dollars in 1850 to one worth sixty million, and with a thousand manufacturers in the United States alone, a half-century later.

Ganong Brothers became part of that trend with G.B. Chocolates, and with another phenomenon of the age, penny candies. An enduring image from that era is of a youngster clutching a few coppers as, under the patient gaze of

The Busy Bees Work for You too

THE chewey centre of many a delighful Ganong confection owes its mellowness to the purest of pure honey.

It is the aim of Ganong Brothers to enhance the virgin purity and exquisite bouquet of well-selected ingredients by expert candy-making.

Over 130 varieties in 42 assortments.

Ganong's
GB
CHOCOLATES

THE GIFT OF GLADNESS

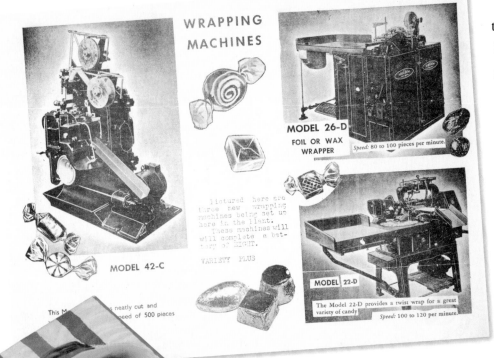

WRAPPING MACHINES

MODEL 42-C

This M[...] neatly cut and [...] speed of 500 pieces.

MODEL 26-D
FOIL OR WAX WRAPPER
Speed: 80 to 100 pieces per minute.

Pictured here are three new wrapping machines being set up here in the plant. These machines will will complete a bat-tery of EIGHT.

VARIETY PLUS

MODEL 22-D
The Model 22-D provides a twist wrap for a great variety of candy.
Speed: 100 to 120 per minute.

Ganong's
GB
Chocolates

the shopkeeper, he deliberately contemplates his choices in a store's cornucopian jars and glass cases. It was a more innocent time, yes, but these discriminating, pint-sized customers were important to business, too. They fueled a resurgence of confectionery staples and kept it going for decades.

At Ganong's, it was an article of faith that three new penny pieces had to be introduced every month and three older ones retired. You had to do that to keep the kids interested. Overall, the company maintained about one hundred and fifty different penny candies — items made with every ingredient and in every shape and size imaginable, and with fetching names like Dudes, Sunbeams, Zoo-Zoos, and the All-Day Sucker. The last was a particularly inspired creation. It consisted of a hard candy ball stuck on the end of a wooden skewer. Ganong's made them in several flavours, and when other companies copied the idea, the All-Day Sucker (its consumption time was actually closer to an hour) became the biggest-selling penny candy in Canada.

As successes like this became more frequent, Gilbert decided, in 1896, to enter federal politics. He ran for Sir John A. Macdonald's old Liberal-Conservative party, and was elected by promising, for example, to build a cold storage facility for Bay of Fundy fishermen using new-fangled refrigeration apparatus like that recently installed in the candy factory — "Mr. Ganong's ice machines," the local weekly called them. He got few chances to speak in the House of

G.W. Ganong campaign ad.

Left: Ganong parade float, celebrating Queen Victoria's Diamond Jubilee, 1897.

Commons, though when he did, he certainly wasn't above earnestly bashing the Liberals, including the Prime Minister, Wilfrid Laurier.

Gilbert would remain in the House for a dozen years. One of his better moments came when he turned fifty on May 22, 1901, and presented each parliamentarian with a package of Ganong's candy. By that time, he was celebrating more than his birthday: company sales were booming, and annual production would reach two and a quarter million pounds that year — enough candy, somebody calculated, to fill a fifty-car freight train.

Then, in March, 1903, a girl lighting a gas jet in the factory basement accidentally ignited a box of celluloid trays. She escaped, but the fire quickly spread to the rest of the building. From the second floor, where the Ganongs maintained living quarters, Maria got out with not much more than the clothes she wore. On the floor above, girls went out windows to the roof, where George Ensor kept several

Fire at the factory, 1903.

from jumping until ladders could be raised for their rescue. Only a firewall kept the flames from spreading into an uninsured new section still under construction.

It was the third fire Gilbert had experienced in thirty years of business. (After the first fire, in 1877, a second blaze, in 1888, had destroyed a new plant he'd put up just two years earlier.) Now he again rebuilt quickly, and the company regained its momentum. By 1913, annual sales were on the doorstep of the million-dollar milestone, and the factory was literally bursting its seams. The real problem now wasn't space, however, but finding the workers to fill it. A partial solution, arrived at a few years earlier, was to

Young employees, 1908;
(top) Starch department, 1904;
(right) store front, circa early 1900s.

Elm Hall residents, 1925.
Eleanor Deacon, the future
Mrs. Whidden Ganong, is eighth
from the left in the second row.
Kings Landing-Ganong Fonds,
Provincial Archives of New Brunswick, P617-1.

open a boarding house so that the company could hire young women from the surrounding countryside while protecting them from the blandishments of a seaport town. The house was a rather elegant Victorian edifice called Elm Hall, and it had a lawn for croquet and a matron with a strict set of rules. For a few years, the company also tried bringing in female workers from Newfoundland and the British Isles, but this worked less well because these girls often lingered just long enough to get their bearings, then took off for the New England states.

For a time, Gilbert actually contemplated moving the company to Saint John, where female labour was in greater supply. He even bought a local candy company, re-christening it Corona. But then the First World War broke out, and with it came new taxes and higher costs for sugar and cocoa beans. Thoughts of relocating the factory faded away (although Corona continued to operate until 1932). Instead, the company added evening hours to the daytime shifts, the first time, outside the pre-Christmas rush, it had ever done that. Among the buyers of all this candy were people who sent chocolates to the boys at the front. And the lads sent back letters of thanks and poignant expressions of how much Ganong's chocolates reminded them of home and better days back in the Maritimes.

Then, in June, 1917, came Gilbert's crowning moment. Years before, he had written in his diary of his aspirations for someday gaining admittance to what he

called "higher society." Now that moment arrived with his appointment as New Brunswick's fourteenth Lieutenant-Governor. He and Maria celebrated with a glittering garden party at Lonicera Hall, the splendid home, named after the wild honeysuckle, they had moved to after the 1903 fire. Unfortunately, it turned out to be not much more than a moment. Four months later, he was felled by a sudden intestinal illness and died.

Gilbert and Maria had no children, so with his passing the company stock went into a trust for his widow, and the business simply carried on. But within this apparently seamless transitional arrangement there lurked a caveat that, later on, would threaten the very continuance of Ganong's as a family enterprise.

Maria Famicha Robinson Ganong.

THE FINE ART OF HAND-DIPPING CHOCOLATES

As far as Gilbert Ganong was concerned, there was only one way to make his company's G.B. Chocolates, and that was by coating every single piece by hand. It was a tedious, exacting process, but it was also one of the ways by which the company built its reputation for quality.

The scene in the turn-of-the century "dipping room" was the stuff of a chocolate-lover's dreams. In a spotlessly white environment, scores of young women wearing white aprons over long dresses and skirts sat at long tables. Beside each was a vat of warm liquid chocolate, from which they scooped enough to maintain a large puddle in front of them. Then they took uncoated candy centres — from caramels to nuts — and one by one drew them through the puddles until each side was coated thickly and uniformly. Now they added a swirl of ornamentation to the tops — each swirl distinctive for the one

Left: Hand cream department, 1910.

hundred and fifty different chocolate pieces Ganong made! Finally, they placed the still-soft pieces on celluloid pads that imprinted the letters G.B.

The process took a long time to learn, even longer to master — it might be five years before a hand-dipper could achieve what were called "perfect goods." But many did learn: by the early 1900s, the company was employing 130 hand-dippers, and over the ensuing years there would be hundreds more. Many were young women from the country, the daughters of farmers, woodsmen, and fishermen. One of them, Eleanor Deacon, became the fastest hand-dipper in the company's history. She would also marry James Ganong's grandson, R. Whidden Ganong, in 1941, after a fourteen-year courtship.

Ganong's Chocolates

Left: the hand-dipping room in 1963.

Below: hand-dipping, the old-fashioned way.

Heritage Management

THE SOLDIERS' BOX

A beautiful new Box of Ganong's **GB** Chocolates

Specially made & packed for sending by mail

The Overseas Box

A box of Ganong's (G.B.) Chocolates specially prepared as a gift box for the soldiers.

FIVE SPECIAL FEATURES:

1—A box of the finest chocolates made with a center-piece of maple cream in the shape of a maple leaf.
2—Each box a Christmas Card Greeting in verse.
3—Specially made to keep well, and specially packed to travel well.
4—The box is so strongly constructed that you can stand on it.
5—Special wrapper with instructions for mailing.

Price, 75 Cents a Box

Ganong's **GB** Chocolates

O. I.

While I was opening the box, Jack Long, my chum, and a German prisoner who is helping him came in and I treated them to, as I said, "some real Canadian chocolates." The German said, "Canadian chocolates are Jake." Now "Jake" is army slang for the finest out, so you can see even a German knows a good thing when he tastes it.

— Private Percy Dolen, First World War.

Chocolate weigh scale, 1920s boxes, copper cooking pot, and tools used for hand-dipping chocolates.

47

MAKE up your own assortment. Add to your hospitality the charm and taste of your own selection.

130 Kinds to choose from!

Ganong's GB Chocolates

Our candies are good to eat, of that I am certain. I eat large quantities every day myself, and so do my associates. Therefore I am not surprised that people eat them. We try to make good eating chocolates that are suited to our Canadian climate. We are proud of all our goods and have never found it necessary to lower the standard to make sales.

— Arthur Ganong, 1906

A TASTE FOR CHOCOLATE

Of all Gilbert Ganong's astute decisions, one of the best, made about the time he went to Ottawa as a Member of Parliament, was to bring his young nephew, James's son Arthur, into the business.

Arthur had been attending the University of New Brunswick in Fredericton when Gilbert hailed him back home to join the family firm. At first, there had been a little disquiet when Arthur, a good athlete, kept playing rugby and getting injured. But then Gilbert sternly informed him that he couldn't expect to be a businessman and play sports, too, especially ones that tended to break parts of his person, and that brought Arthur's budding athletic career to a sudden and premature end.

Thereafter, he diligently applied himself to his work. It so happened that he had arrived in the business at the same moment, more or less, that chocolate became the confectionery industry's bellwether. Arthur was drawn to the whole exotic aura surrounding chocolate — its long history, how the beans were harvested in places like Trinidad and Brazil and Ceylon, how each country's beans were different, had a distinctive taste, colour, and quality, and how choosing the right ones to blend was critical to the success or failure of the finished product. This interest, which evolved into an expertise, became especially important after 1906, when Ganong's decided that the only way to ensure consistently high quality was to mix its own chocolate and installed the necessary equipment. Maintaining standards was how you beat the competition, the Ganongs insisted, and so the one thing never compromised, in good time or bad down through the decades, was chocolate quality.

Arthur Ganong as a student at the University of New Brunswick, 1896.

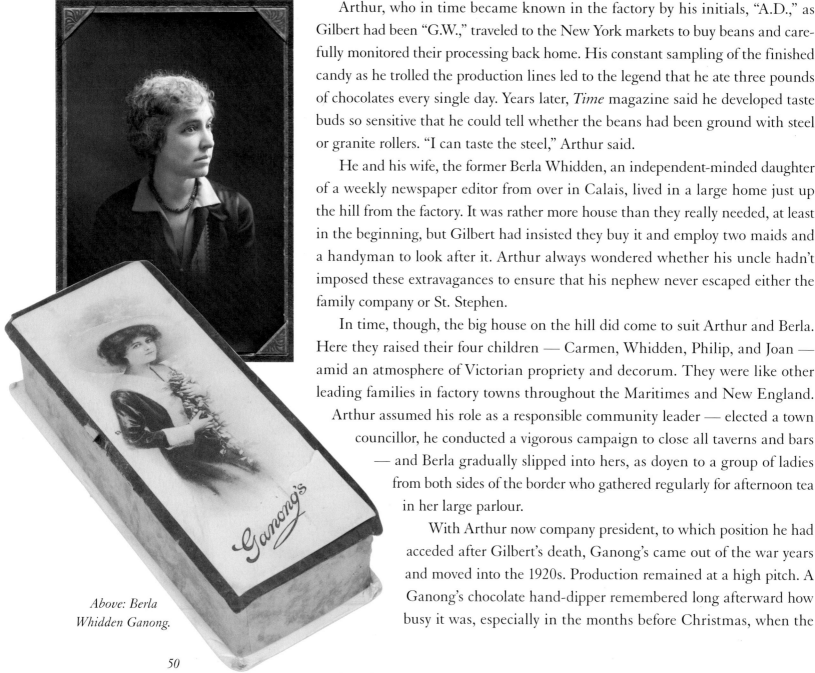

Above: Berla Whidden Ganong.

Arthur, who in time became known in the factory by his initials, "A.D.," as Gilbert had been "G.W.," traveled to the New York markets to buy beans and carefully monitored their processing back home. His constant sampling of the finished candy as he trolled the production lines led to the legend that he ate three pounds of chocolates every single day. Years later, *Time* magazine said he developed taste buds so sensitive that he could tell whether the beans had been ground with steel or granite rollers. "I can taste the steel," Arthur said.

He and his wife, the former Berla Whidden, an independent-minded daughter of a weekly newspaper editor from over in Calais, lived in a large home just up the hill from the factory. It was rather more house than they really needed, at least in the beginning, but Gilbert had insisted they buy it and employ two maids and a handyman to look after it. Arthur always wondered whether his uncle hadn't imposed these extravagances to ensure that his nephew never escaped either the family company or St. Stephen.

In time, though, the big house on the hill did come to suit Arthur and Berla. Here they raised their four children — Carmen, Whidden, Philip, and Joan — amid an atmosphere of Victorian propriety and decorum. They were like other leading families in factory towns throughout the Maritimes and New England. Arthur assumed his role as a responsible community leader — elected a town councillor, he conducted a vigorous campaign to close all taverns and bars — and Berla gradually slipped into hers, as doyen to a group of ladies from both sides of the border who gathered regularly for afternoon tea in her large parlour.

With Arthur now company president, to which position he had acceded after Gilbert's death, Ganong's came out of the war years and moved into the 1920s. Production remained at a high pitch. A Ganong's chocolate hand-dipper remembered long afterward how busy it was, especially in the months before Christmas, when the

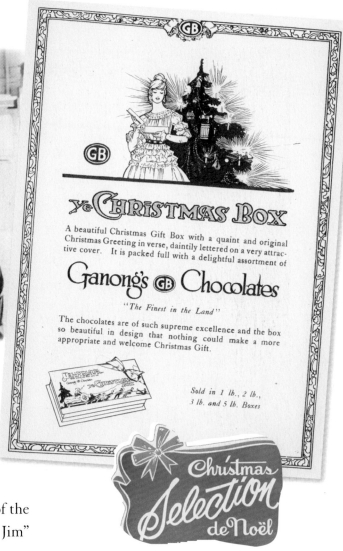

factory whistle sounded over St. Stephen at seven in the morning, you worked until six at night, then went back for three more hours in the evening. There wasn't much daylight in your life. But it was also candy's romantic era. Advertising blossomed, window dressers erected elegant displays, and shops, drugstores, even restaurants stacked their shelves, counters, and glass cases with chocolates in beautifully illustrated boxes.

In St. Stephen, Ganong Brothers had a store of their own at the front of the factory. A dedicated, if slightly eccentric, family cousin named "Cinnamon Jim" Ganong presided over it, spending most of his waking hours there. In the evenings, after he'd locked the door and turned the lights out, he'd often just sit inside the store in the dark and watch how life in postwar Canada unfolded on his small town's main street.

Left: Packing coconut bonbons in wooden tubs, 1910.

INVENTING THE CHOCOLATE BAR

One of the many candy pieces that came out of the Ganong factory in the early part of the twentieth century was the world's first five-cent chocolate nut bar. How it happened is a Canadian legend involving Arthur Ganong and his wife Berla, their children, candy-maker George Ensor, and a Jersey cow with a stubborn streak.

The cow was one of three Arthur kept on his property, just uphill from the factory. The animals were usually tethered on the front lawn,

A.D. Ganong and his children.

Streetcar sign for the original nut bar.

GANONG'S *Evangeline*

THE ORIGINAL NUT BAR IS DELICIOUS CHOCOLATE NUT BAR

and when it came time for them to go to the barn, this particular one always resisted. So Berla resorted to a trick: when the factory whistle sounded at the end of the day, she would rush outside and untether the balky animal. Seeing Arthur coming up the front walk, the cow would then obligingly chase him into the barn.

So amusing was this daily scene to the Ganong children that they urged their father to make some chocolate for them using the Jersey's milk. Arthur recruited George Ensor to the task, and together they mixed the milk chocolate with nuts and moulded it into long strips. The pieces were a hit with the children. Arthur and George liked them, too, and they began carrying them on fishing trips into the New Brunswick woods. Finally, in 1910, they put them on the market — and the world had its first five-cent chocolate nut bar.

The original candy bar blossomed into many variations. Advertising and wrappers from the 1950s.

James Ganong's sons, 1895:
(standing) Walter and Edwin;
(seated) Will and Arthur.

A TALENTED GENERATION

Arthur Ganong wasn't the only talented family member of his generation. In fact, all six of James Ganong's children did rather well for themselves. Edwin made a success of the soap company. Walter, another son, taught electrical engineering and then ran the Ganong Brothers subsidiary, the Corona Company, of Saint John. Daughter Katherine married a Baptist minister, Howard Whidden, later president of Manitoba's Brandon University and a Member of Parliament. Another daughter, Susan, bought the Netherwood School for Girls, in Rothesay, New Brunswick, and served as its principal for more than four decades.

And then there was the oldest boy, Will — Dr. William Francis Ganong. He became a professor of botany at Smith College in Massachusetts, a distinguished scientist, writer, and historian. Not inclined toward business, unlike his brothers, he nonetheless played an important role in the fortunes of the candy company. When, in the 1930s, a dispute arose over ownership, the minutes he'd meticulously kept of company meetings over the years proved an invaluable record.

Another way in which Will helped was as an occasional boon companion for Arthur when the latter, seeking release from the strain of managing the family firm in difficult times, set out on excursions into the wilds of New Brunswick. The two were on a wilderness junket when Will decided to name the province's highest mountain, Mount Carleton, after its first governor. Later, he also introduced Arthur's young

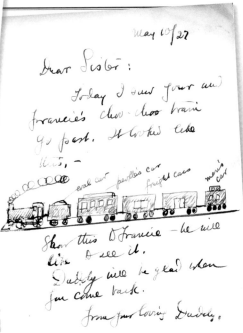

May 14/27

Dear Sister :

Mummy says you are a good girl, and are having a good time, and Daddy is glad.

See if you know what this is, and whose it is.

Your loving Daddy.

May 10/27

Dear Sister :

Today I saw your and Francie's choo-choo train go past. It looked like this, —

coal car   peoples car   fright cars   men's car

Show this to Francie — he will like to see it.
Daddy will be glad when you come back.

from your loving Daddy.

William Francis Ganong, 1895.

Left: notes from William F. Ganong to his children, vacationing in Iowa with their mother.

son Whidden (a future company president) to the rigours of wilderness life.

While Will earned renown at Smith as both a scientist and a teacher, every summer for thirty-seven years he came back to New Brunswick, where he researched its natural and human history. He wrote and published prolifically on these subjects. An admiring colleague called him "the greatest authority who ever lived" on the province.

Right: Will Ganong and his wife Anna on a field trip in New Brunswick, 1923.

H.W.B Smith Fonds, Provincial Archives of New Brunswick, P-616-1-9

Examples of Ganong packaging, from lithographed tin pails of the early 1900s to a 1980s Christmas tree box.

THE ART OF SELLING CANDY

Confectionery wasn't the only field in which Ganong Brothers was innovative. The company was also a Canadian pioneer in advertising and marketing, and its vintage poster and magazine advertisements, and the illustrated boxes in which it packaged its chocolates over the decades, constitute their own unique social legacy.

Gilbert Ganong, of course, early on learned the value of putting his message before the public. Even when he was just starting out in business, he would sometimes reward the editor of the hometown *Saint Croix Courier* with a basket of fruit in return for a favourable mention in the newspaper's columns.

By the late nineteenth century, advertising, which had once been a field largely left to flamboyant circus promoters and patent medicine salesmen, was evolving into a more refined and sophisticated business: As consumerism blossomed, manufacturers like Ganong's sought new and better ways to promote and sell their wares.

An important technological change was the development of colour process printing around the turn of the century. Just as it transformed book and magazine publishing, so, too, did it usher in a new era in advertising. And among those who benefited most were artists who, during this golden age of illustration, obtained lucrative commissions to create lush and elegant advertisements for products as wide-ranging

as men's shirts and railway travel. Nearly all of Canada's famous Group of Seven, for example, did turns as commercial artists.

Ganong's found a niche for its illustrated colour advertisements on Canadian streetcars. As a highly visible symbol of the company's determination to have a national presence, the ads have to be seen in the context of when they appeared — the middle years of the twentieth century's second decade — and where. There was no television then, no radio, and Canadian consumer magazines were still relatively new. But the Toronto streetcar system, which had started as a horse-drawn affair in 1861, had long since progressed to an electrified transit network that each day carried thousands of passengers. Sitting on the cars' crimson-cushioned seats, the commuters had only to lift their eyes to see the evocative posters promoting Ganong's chocolates on the wall opposite.

The ads were rich in Edwardian idealism. The women were lovely, the men handsome. They were shown as fashionable couples enjoying the simple pleasures of the age: fishing, canoeing, horseback riding, and sliding on the pristine snows of a Canadian winter. Of course, romance was in the air, and a box of Ganong's chocolates was always at hand to smooth its way.

How important were these streetcar posters or "cards" to an up-and-coming confectioner? Important enough that sometimes several different ones were created on a common theme, so that they could be changed periodically in the course of a year. There was a seasonal series, a Shakespeare series, and so forth. A memorandum about the company's advertising referred to the posters as the "heavy artillery" of any campaign. "The cards must not only be striking and effective in themselves,"

Some of the many streetcar advertisements produced by Ganong's.

In no other advertising (except perhaps, the advertising of fashions) is it so important to have the highest grade of drawings and the very best taste in design and display.

— *Memo regarding Ganong's chocolate campaign, 1915*

He who cares is careful. He chooses Ganong's for wholesome quality and delicious flavor.

Ganong's GB Chocolates

Opening the Spring Campaign with a box of GANONG'S

Ganong's GB

GANONG'S
THE FINEST GB IN THE LAND
CHOCOLATES

"TO THE VICTOR BELONG THE SPOILS

G.B's FOR THE BO

"Love's Labor Lost"

GANONG'S
THE FINEST GB IN THE LAND
CHOCOLATES

it said, "but must also sound the keynote for all the other advertising matter that appears at the same time."

Later, in the 1930s, the company sounded much the same message when it made full-page, full-colour ads in *Maclean's* centrepieces of its selling campaigns. By then, *Maclean's* had become a new force in the Canadian marketplace. A few years earlier, the magazine had produced a national survey showing that the people who owned automobiles were essentially the same ones who read *Maclean's* — in other words, a cohort of middle-class consumer families with disposable income. It was precisely the same group that Ganong's needed to reach to sell its chocolates. So, at Easter, 1930, only a few months after the Great Depression began, the company bought a full-page ad for the Delecto brand. Copies of the ad also went to salesmen and storekeepers with a message urging them to tie window displays to the magazine campaign. "Over 800,000 people will see this advertisement," they were told, "and increased sales are bound to result for dealers who link their store with this national advertising campaign, for it will reach prospects in every part of the Dominion."

These prospects included customers who spoke French and lived in places like northern New Brunswick, Quebec, and Manitoba, and so, early on, the company created French advertising and promotional materials. There were full-page advertisements in French-language magazines, and the collector cards in the Big Chief chocolate bars of the 1930s were bilingual.

THE NEW BIG FLAT BOX
Ganong's Touring Special
This Assortment is a selection of the
six most popular of - Ganong's GB Chocolates

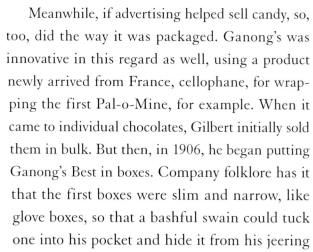

"It may be a Scrap of Paper, but I'll fight for it"

Meanwhile, if advertising helped sell candy, so, too, did the way it was packaged. Ganong's was innovative in this regard as well, using a product newly arrived from France, cellophane, for wrapping the first Pal-o-Mine, for example. When it came to individual chocolates, Gilbert initially sold them in bulk. But then, in 1906, he began putting Ganong's Best in boxes. Company folklore has it that the first boxes were slim and narrow, like glove boxes, so that a bashful swain could tuck one into his pocket and hide it from his jeering pals as he went to call on a young lady. Packaging, whatever its size, was an instant hit, and that same year Ganong's established the Home Paper Box Company to make chocolate boxes right in its own factory.

It was the beginning of another form of social history, for the illustrated box covers often reflected the period when they were used. In times of war, for example, the pastoral scenes of peacetime gave way to wrappers that depicted fighting ships at sea and a sturdy English bulldog rampant on a fluttering Union Jack. Not always were the motifs successful, however. A memorable mistake occurred during the First World War, when the company put out a box whose wrapper showed an empty rocking chair beside a fireplace, a reminder of absent sons, husbands, and fathers, and one that was simply too poignant; the box did not sell.

Usually, though, the topical boxes were popular, and they could be adaptable, too. For people who needed a practical reason for buying chocolates during the Great Depression, for example, Ganong's created a "box" that doubled as a sewing basket, and another made of wood and shaped like a small cedar chest for storing mementoes.

There were, in fact, all kinds of boxes over the years, fancy ones and simple ones, Christmas boxes and heart-shaped Valentine boxes, the latter an innovation that Ganong's introduced to Canada in the 1930s. Flowers, Gibson Girls, silent film stars, and hunting tableaux were all subjects for Ganong's boxes — by the late 1950s, the box factory was making eighty-three different packages. Many of the wrappers for the boxes were provided by a tall, courtly Englishman, A.V. Mansell, who arrived at the factory each year with a portfolio of colourful scenes and then lingered in St. Stephen for two or three days while the company made its choices.

Above right: the Home Paper Box Company.

It was Mansell who sold Ganong's on using a coach and horses, and a colour scheme of blue and gold, to illustrate the Delecto brand of boxed chocolates. He recommended it because, at his printing plant in London, he used a gold ink that wouldn't tarnish. The coach theme was the right elegant touch for Ganong's top-of-the-line chocolates, and it stayed on the Delecto box for nearly three decades, before being abandoned in the 1970s in favour of a more contemporary design.

The "Sheik Tells the Story" series was one of the earliest bilingual advertising campaigns by Ganong's. Ads were published across Canada in 1927.

Ganong's
GB
Chocolates

Le Charme
PACKAGE

ONE
LB.
NET

Ganong's
GB
Chocolates

The finest
in the
land

Ganong's GB Chocolates

FROM ST. STEPHEN, WITH LOVE

In the 1930s, when the country needed a pick-me-up, Ganong's introduced the heart-shaped box of chocolates to Canada. They made their debut at the Paradise restaurant and Wasson drugstores in Saint John, New Brunswick — as a Christmas item! It wasn't long, though, before somebody recognized that the boxes really belonged with Valentine's Day, and thus was born a Ganong — and a Canadian — tradition.

Created in a more expressive time, the showy Valentine boxes, shaped in red cardboard on wooden forms in the fourth-floor box factory, were the antithesis of the minimalist packages that had once been romantic currency. In time, all sorts of decorative flourishes were added, and women on the production line fussed over every single box to get the ribbons and ruffles straight. Valentine's Day became the biggest single day in the whole year for selling chocolates, bigger even than Easter and Mother's Day. Ganong's alone sometimes offered as many as fifty different palpitations of the heart. There were large boxes and small, boxes for kids and for aspiring lovers, elegant boxes with gold leaf and mauve ribbons, and others that were simply gussied up, a box with a man's tuxedo front on its cover, and another that depicted a comely vintage garden scene.

No Ganong's employee ever embraced it all more keenly than Jim Purcell. A man of unbridled enthusiasm, he had originally been hired, so the story went, because another employee, Bill Cleghorn, who managed the hometown baseball team, didn't want to lose his hard-hitting first baseman. Rising through Ganong's ranks to become a vice-president, Purcell brought to all his assignments the same energy and dedication he applied to selling Valentine chocolates. Dubbed the "Valentine King of Canada" by industry colleagues, he explained it this way: "With all the hatred in the world today, it's nice to sell love."

Right: James W. Purcell, vice-president of production, 1976. He made it a personal mission to sell Valentine chocolates.

A wooden mold (shown at right) was used to shape the original heart-shaped boxes introduced by Ganong's in the 1930s. The company went on to invent a delightful number of novelty Valentine boxes.

SWEET EVANGELINE

She was the perfect symbol for a candy company, manifesting virtues of purity and excellence and inspiring thoughts of romance and courtship. Evangeline, the tragic heroine from the famous narrative poem by Henry Wadsworth Longfellow, represented ideally the aspirations and aura surrounding the Ganong company and its products.

A long tradition existed of chocolate companies choosing depictions of lovely young women to grace their packages and advertising. Ganong's chose Evangeline, in 1904, because she was, as Arthur Ganong said, "an outstanding representation of the Maritimes."

Although Longfellow had written *Evangeline, A Tale of Acadie* more than half a century earlier, the work was more popular than ever. Every school child knew the story of Evangeline and the Acadian Expulsion, and each year

thousands of visitors traveled to Grand Pré, Nova Scotia, site of the deportation in 1755.

To capture Evangeline's sweet persona, Ganong's commissioned a painting by John David Kelly, a Canadian artist known for his depictions of the nation's historical figures and scenes (including, coincidentally, the settling of the United Empire Loyalists in Saint John). Kelly's image of Evangeline was used in Ganong's sales materials and advertising. There were also Evangeline boxed chocolates and an Evangeline cream bar. And the company put the Acadian heroine on its letterhead, where she remained, demure and ageless, until the late 1970s.

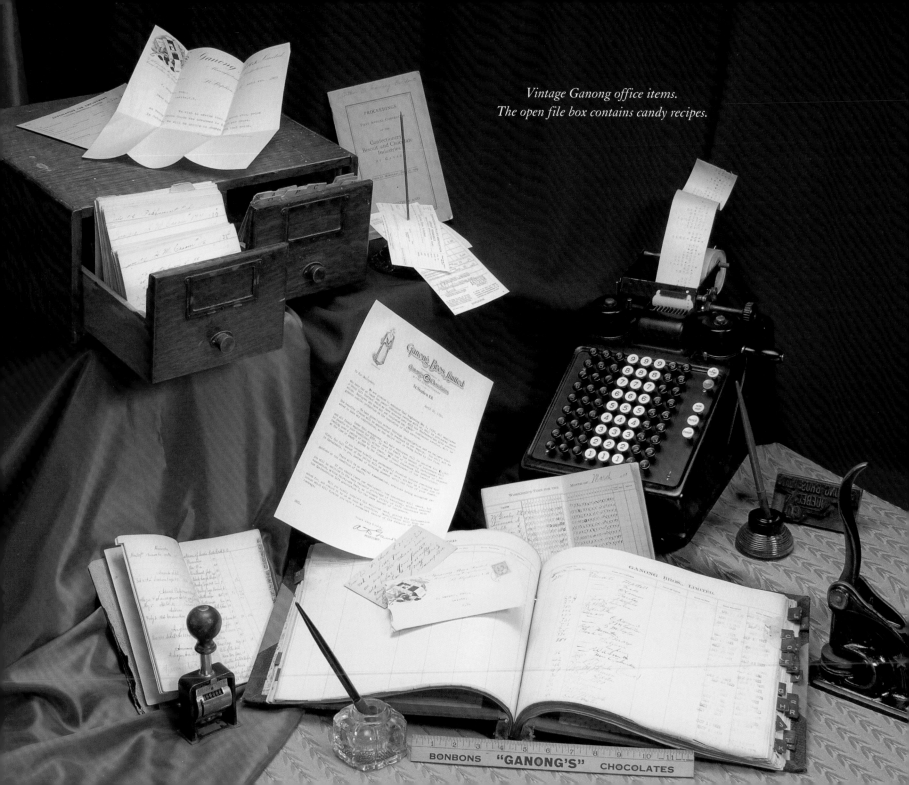

Vintage Ganong office items.
The open file box contains candy recipes.

SAVING THE COMPANY

On March 9, 1929, George Ensor died. As factory superintendent, the old Baltimore candy-maker had been a Ganong's stalwart, and his passing left a large void. That evening, during a long walk, Arthur's son Whidden asked his father whom he had in mind to take over Ensor's job. Arthur replied that it would probably be a family cousin named Hardy Ganong. Whidden responded, "There is someone you are overlooking," and when Arthur asked whom that might be, his son boldly declared: "Me."

Arthur wasn't keen on the idea. He thought that Whidden, just twenty-two and barely two years in the business, was far too young and inexperienced. But on the morning after Ensor's funeral, Whidden went to the factory before anybody else and took over the superintendent's office. In a way, he never left it.

Whidden (from his mother's maiden name) was the consummate factory man. Even years later, after he'd become company president, his heart was still out there on the production lines. He made a point of greeting each worker as he or she arrived in the morning, and of bidding each good night at the end of the day. He loved the factory, where, in time, like his father and Gilbert, he, too, came to be known by his initials, "Mr. R.W."

But no moment in the factory ever made more of an impression on him than those first months after he took over the superintendent's job. The period leading up to Christmas that year was like a last shining moment before the company, and the rest of the world, plunged into the depths of the Great Depression. The rush began immediately after Labour Day, when the factory stepped up production

R.W. Ganong, circa 1945.

Right: state-of-the-art adding machine at the Ganong offices, circa 1930.

of items for the Christmas trade. Nearly two-thirds of the output for the entire year was produced in those few months. Many seasonal workers were brought in, and the company roster jumped from three hundred employees to seven hundred. Hours were extended to include four evenings a week and Saturday afternoons.

The scene was like a cross between a fantasyland and something out of Dickens. Huge amounts of chocolates, chocolate bars, creams, jellies, gumdrops and jellybeans were produced. There was a "barley toy corner" where people made nothing but "clear toys," and another place where six "master candy pullers" crafted ribbon candy and striped candy canes. Other candy-makers turned out pink Chicken Bones and multi-coloured mixtures of hard candies that were then packed in wooden tubs or crates or lithographed tin pails for shipment to stores all over the Dominion. Amid this frenetic scene, scores of boys and girls, some as young as fourteen, worked as starch-drenched helpers. It *was* a little Dickensian, but for an ambitious young person, it was also the sort of place where one could start a meaningful career. That's what happened to a lad named Eldon Libby. He came off the farm, and George Ensor, spotting some essential traits, took him under wing. Libby went on to become assistant factory superintendent and, eventually, head candy-maker. With the company for half a century, he would invent hundreds of distinctive candy pieces.

As the Depression began, there was still an air of confidence mingling with the sweet fragrances of the Ganong factory. But, by the end of 1932, candy production in Canada was off by more than thirty percent, and Ganong's sales were less than half of their level before the Depression. The company closed its Toronto sales office and cut wages and salaries at the factory.

Then a new crisis arose. Gilbert's widow Maria died, throwing the whole issue of company succession and ownership into

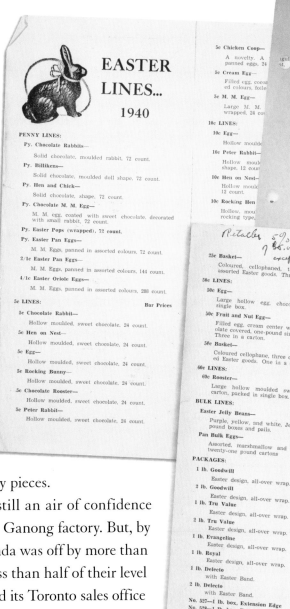

Sales brochures and a notebook showing production figures for an Easter product.

Eldon Libby, assistant superintendent and chief candy man from 1930 to 1971.

dispute. The problem was that, at his death seventeen years earlier, Gilbert had not spelled out how the business was to be continued. Maria had simply inherited all of her husband's stock, and it was placed in a trust. But the trust agreement, which gave Arthur and his three brothers proxy on the shares, specified that it was to remain in effect only as long as the company could pay Maria a dividend. By 1934, that was becoming impossible. So Arthur and his brothers, not long before Maria's death, had approached her about making a new arrangement. Accepting the view of a trusted advisor, she turned them down.

Maria's advisor in this and other financial matters was a man named Sam McBride. He seemed to resent the Ganongs who followed Gilbert — he felt they had inherited rather than earned their status — and he focused his criticism on poor, beleaguered Arthur. Now, as executor of Maria's estate, McBride had effectively gained control of the company.

A team of consultants later added more fuel to the fire by reporting the factory's operation too lax and management's treatment of employees too generous. Unless things changed, the consultants said, the company could go bankrupt. And not much had escaped their steely gaze, it seemed, not even the romantic interests of Whidden, then in the midst of his fourteen-year courtship of one of the factory girls. Summoning him to the office one evening, a consultant told Whidden to end the romance because it was bad form. Whidden promptly promised to throw the man out a factory window if the matter were ever raised again. It wasn't.

While Arthur sought compromise on some of the consultants' cost-cutting recommendations, Sam McBride wanted them followed nearly to the letter. He also blocked proposals to buy new equipment. It was a frustrating, impossible stand-off that was resolved only when the matter finally went to court. Using his carefully kept company minutes, Will Ganong prepared a cogent paper on the complicated evolution of the firm's ownership, and when the case wound up with the Privy Council in England, the Ganongs won.

There remained one more dramatic moment in this whole affair. It came at the end of the Second World War, when Whidden, back from the service, took it upon himself to persuade distant family relatives, to whom Maria's stock had gone after the Privy Council decision, to sell it back to Arthur and his siblings. Most agreed, and a shareholders' meeting was scheduled for April, 1946. At that meeting, Sam McBride reappeared and, with backing from the McLean family, who owned Connors Bros., a nearby fish-packing company, entered a bid that was far more than the Ganongs could afford to counter.

Only an impish bit of last-minute play-acting and emotional entreaty by Whidden saved the day. Meeting in his office with two distant Ganong cousins after a twenty-four-hour reprieve, Whidden faked a telephone call in which a banker ostensibly denied him the money needed to match the McLean-McBride bid. Then he passionately, and convincingly, told the cousins of the personal sacrifices his father had made to keep the company afloat. A short time later, the cousins swung their considerable blocks of shares to the Ganongs. The next day, Arthur called all the plant employees together and proudly told them that Whidden had rescued the company.

Ganong "float" for a Calgary parade, 1934.

"THAT'S CANDY"

● A worker in a munitions
plant. It's mid-afternoon. He's tiring.
The day is starting to drag. He stops. Reaches into his
pocket and takes out some GANONG'S (G.B.) CHOCOLATES.
Takes a bite, relishes the delicious wholesome flavor,
takes another bite and grins. Is cheered, is braced with
every bite. Goes back to his work. Is happier and more
efficient in his task.

"THAT'S CANDY"

Ganong's GB Chocolates

GANONG BROS., LIMITED ～ ST. STEPHEN, N. B.

GANONG BROTHERS, LIMITED

PROXY

I, being
of
a shareholder of Ganong Brothers, Limited, do hereby appoint Arthur
D. Ganong of Saint Stephen, New Brunswick, or failing him, A.
Brewer Edwards of Saint Stephen, New Brunswick, or failing him,

, as my proxy
of
to vote for me and on my behalf at a special general meeting of the
shareholders of Ganong Brothers, Limited, to be held on Monday,
June 17, 1946, and at any adjournment thereof.

As witness my hand this

day of June 1946.

_____

_____
Witness

GANONG BROTHERS, LIMITED

NOTICE IS HEREBY GIVEN that a Special General Meeting of
the shareholders of Ganong Brothers, Limited, will be held at the
office of the Company in Saint Stephen, New Brunswick, on Monday,
June 17, 1946, at Two o'clock in the afternoon for the purpose of
considering, and if thought fit, sanctioning, with or without modifica-
tion, a by-law of the Company enacted by the Directors on May 28,
1946, in the words, letters and figures following:—

"Be it enacted and it is hereby enacted as a by-law of the Company,

1. That subject to confirmation by Supplementary Letters
Patent the name of the Company be and the same is hereby changed
to Gilwhite Limited.

2. That upon this by-law having been sanctioned by the shareholders of the Company, an application for Supplementary Letters
Patent confirming the change of name be and the same is hereby
authorized."

and to transact such other business as may properly come before the
meeting.

Dated at Saint Stephen, New Brunswick, this fifth day of June,
1946.

By order of the Board.

J. H. DRUMMIE, Secretary.

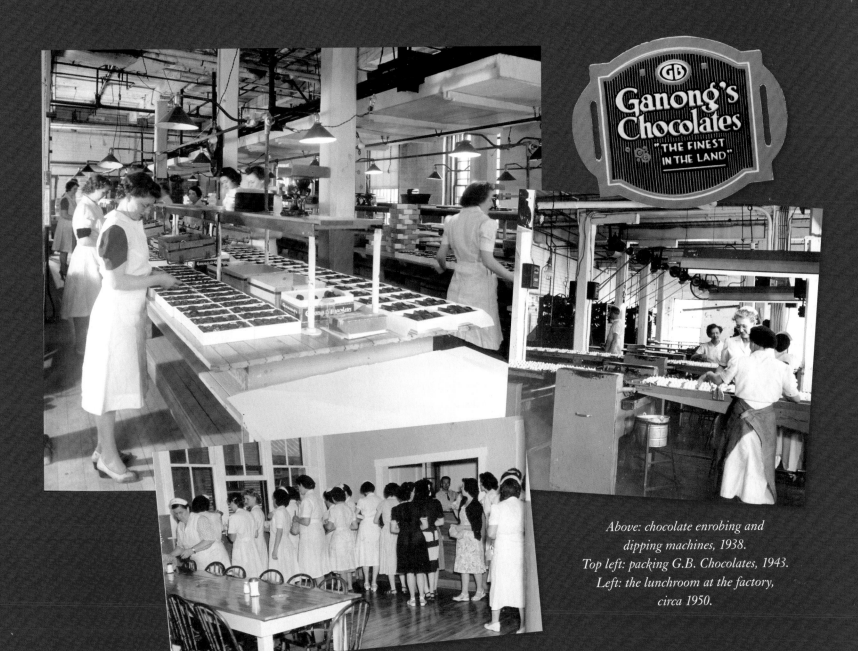

*Above: chocolate enrobing and
dipping machines, 1938.
Top left: packing G.B. Chocolates, 1943.
Left: the lunchroom at the factory,
circa 1950.*

NOON DAY,
CHIPPEWAY.

LEAN WOLF,
GROS VENTRES.

MANY HORNS,
BLACKFEET SIOUX.

THE BIG CHIEF BAR

In the early decades of the twentieth century, the public was fascinated by "American Indians" and their relationship with the natural world, and it undoubtedly pleased Whidden Ganong and his father Arthur, avid outdoorsmen both, that the family business had a product that celebrated them.

Inside the wrapper of each Big Chief bar was a collector card bearing a full-colour picture of a Native leader. There were fifty of these cards, each with a bilingual message on the back urging Big Chief aficionados to collect the whole set so they could play an "Indian game."

Collector cards were not a new phenomenon. Cigarette manufacturers had been issuing them since the nineteenth century, and many of the major chocolate companies eventually followed. Ganong's themselves produced a second series, this one with a rodeo theme.

But the Big Chief cards, based on portraits at the U.S. Department of the Interior in Washington, D.C., seem to have been the family favourite. Whidden Ganong remembered having, at age fifteen, a complete set of the cards, which he tacked up on the wall of a family fishing camp.

Big Chief and Rodeo bar collector cards.

THE OVERLAND MAIL

AN OLD-TIME COWBOY

RIDING A BUFFALO

RED BIRD,
CHIPPEWAY.

MAN AND CHIEF,
PAWNEE

CROW'S BREAST,
GROS VENTRES.

THE LARIAT DANCE

RIDING A STEER

12
GANONG'S "RODEO" BARS
What does "RODEO" mean?
YIP! YIP! YIP!
THE COWBOY AND THE WILD WEST...
A Regular Wild West Show
50 THRILLING PICTURES
of Cowboy Life and Hair Raising Stunts
Every Picture a Dandy
50 - GET THEM ALL - 50
and don't forget
GANONG'S FOR QUALITY

LES BARRES "RODEO"
Que signifie "RODEO"?
YIP! YIP! YIP!
LE COWBOY ET L'OUEST SAUVAGE...
un spectacle régulier du Grand-Ouest
50 IMAGES SENSATIONNELLES
à faire dresser les cheveux, de la vie du Cowboy
Chaque image est une trouvaille.
Procurez-vous toutes les 50.
Et n'oubliez pa
GANONG

Ganong's BARS AND ROLLS

5¢

Ganong's
GB Chocolates

Truly the "Gift of Gladness" . . . five pounds of "Ganong's Best", packaged in its regular box, overwrapped with a red seasonal wrap.

Ganong's
GB
CHOCOLATES

Delecto — Canada's Finest Gift Package of Chocolates

Famous "DELECTO" . . . the greatest in chocolate quality now in a new traditionally distinctive package — available in one, two, three and five pound boxes — a beautiful new presentation.

EN • NEW BRUNSWICK

"GOLD RUSH" — a new brand and exciting "Gold Rush" design — beautiful quality chocolates — lovely to open, containing taste sensations which will appeal to every customer.

"C'EST POUR VOUS" — a new and very appealing box for our French friends. "C'est pour vous" . . . the English version, "It's for you".

Sales catalogues, circa 1960.

86

CHOCOLATS GB GANO

$\mathcal{S}$oyez à la page.... en offrant ce qu'il y a de meilleur, il n'y a pas d'erreur possible. Les chocolats Ganong sont le choix parfait, tout indiqué, pour vos amis, votre hôtesse, vos invités. Les centres Ganong sont recueillis de tous les coins du globe. Ensuite, ils sont enrobés du plus délicieux chocolat, pour que vous puissiez les offrir à des connaisseurs. Chacun sait que les chocolats Ganong sont ce qu'il y a de meilleur au pays.

Un de ces jours — bientôt nous l'espérons — nous aurions des Ganong chaque fois que vous en demanderez.

Chocolats GB Ganong

Ce qu'il y a de meilleur au pays!
GANONG BROS. LIMITED, ST-STEPHEN, N.B.

Bienvenu comme la première bouffée de printemps...

un cadeau de
Ganong

"Les meilleurs au pays"

Les bonbons sont nutritifs, mangez-en souvent!

GANONG BROS. LIM
St-Stephen,

Above: An ad from La Presse, March 1953. Ganongs advertised in French publications as early as the 1920s.

TIME OF TRANSITION

With the ownership issue finally resolved in 1946, Ganong's looked forward to a rosy future. The Great Depression and the Second World War had added up to a decade and a half of pent-up indulgence, and who could benefit more from its long-awaited release than a candy company? Ganong's regrouped, reorganized, and undertook an overdue refurbishing of the factory. And when, in 1948, the rationing of cocoa and sugar came to an end, prospects looked brighter still.

But, as Gilbert Ganong had once confided to his diary, each year brought its surprises, no matter how experienced in business one was. In 1950, one of those surprises came in the form of a thirty percent excise tax that the federal government imposed on confectionery.

It was a devastating blow to the industry, and at Ganong's it made a casualty of one of the company's most popular candies, a chocolate "bar" called Pepts. This marked the beginning of a struggle that Ganong's, and other confectioners, would wage for another twenty-five years. It was not until

Above: the company building, circa 1950

1975 that Ottawa finally removed the excise tax from candy and chocolates.

The demise of Pepts showed that the industry was actually far from being comfortably static. In fact, everything was changing. Companies were getting bigger, competition was getting keener. There were new ways of marketing and selling. For Arthur Ganong, a lot of it struck him as rather, well, unseemly.

At Ganong's, a basic philosophy had always been: make a quality product, and the world will find you. So the company had approached marketing with a certain gentlemanly delicacy. It resisted stocking Delecto boxed chocolates with the new grocery chains because it didn't want to offend its traditional retail outlets, the drugstores. Arthur also refused to embrace bagged candies, a product of the automation that was sweeping the industry. Bagged candies just didn't have the same quality, he would say, and he lost valuable ground to the competition.

At the same time, Arthur was experiencing poignant personal changes. His elder daughter, Carmen, died in 1956, and, barely a year and a half later, Berla passed away. Then, in the spring of 1960, he lost his closest business confidante, Brewer Edwards, a fifty-year veteran with Ganong's. Arthur had already relinquished the company presidency to Whidden in 1957, and made a vice-president of his younger son, Philip, who left the firm not long afterward. Still, the old man went to the office every day, and maintained such undiminished independence at home that he steadfastly refused Whidden's offer to come over in the late evenings and stoke the wood furnace for him. In early August, 1960, he celebrated his eighty-third birthday. Then, a few months later, he, too, was gone.

Cellophane packaging machine, 1962.

THE SAD DEMISE OF PEPTS

People loved the Pepts bar for all kinds of reasons, beginning with the fact that it really wasn't a bar in the conventional sense. It consisted of several chocolate-coated peppermint-cream pieces individually wrapped in foil, which allowed mothers to dispense them to their children one at a time. They were a preferred snack of movie-goers, too, because their foil wrappers made them relatively noiseless in a hushed theatre. And there was also the name, which implied a certain peptic benefit.

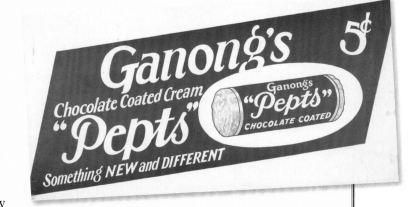

Apart from booming sales, which kept forty to fifty employees at the factory doing nothing but hand-wrapping Pepts, the bar also gave the company the advantage of being able to vary the number of pieces according to prevailing costs — during the Depression, for example, when cocoa beans were just four and a half cents a pound, Ganong Brothers could pack twelve pieces in a five-cent bar and still make money.

But the 1950 excise tax was too much. Unlike regular chocolate bars, which could be subtly slimmed down to save money, the cut forced on Pepts was too drastic, and the bar died. The post-war period, it seemed, wouldn't be entirely sweetness and light after all.

Ganong's
GB
CHOCOLATES

GANONG BROS. LTD
ST. STEPHEN, N.B. CANADA

ONE POUND NET WEIGHT

MAPLE LEAF

FOOD CONTAINER
CONTENTS
12 BISCUIT RATION
2 CHOCOLATE RATION
12 MILK CHOCOLATE
TABLET RATION
THIS IS CONCENTRATED FOOD
& SHOULD BE EATEN SLOWLY

LIFEBOAT & RAFT
RATION

LIFEBOAT & RAFT
RATION

32

CHOCOLATE INCLUDED IN NEW SHIPWRECK SAILOR RATION

CHOCOLATE tablets and bars are included in the newest type ration of all . . . the "shipwreck ration", which has been devised by the Canadian Naval Headquarters.

Each emergency ration kit, no bigger than a woman's overnight case, will hold eight 16-ounce tins of water, eight tins of high caloric food and eight packets of sealed milk tablets. Four of the kits will be fastened to each ten-man raft.

The food tin (as illustrated) is slightly larger than a sardine can and holds 12 chocolate tablets, two chocolate bars, and concentrated biscuits.

Good candy, one of the best foods, is highly nutritious. Quality chocolates and chocolate bars supply the greatest amount of nourishment in the smallest possible bulk.

NOTE.—This advertisement is not meant to imply that Canadian Naval Headquarters have selected or endorsed Ganong's products. It is merely intended to show that quality chocolate bars and chocolates are wholesome and nourishing.

Ganong's
CHOCOLATES
Delecto package

Ganong's
CHOCOLATES
Trevalue

Ganong's
CLOVER MILK
CHOCOLATE
SOLID MILK CHOCOLATE

Ganong's
GB
Chocolates

GANONG BROS. LTD. ST. STEPHEN, N.B.

Ganong's
GB
Chocolates

ONWARD PACKAGE
ONE POUND NET

*Right: Whidden with his nephew
David Ganong, circa 1970.*

By now, Ganong's was in the middle of a long period — one that would last into the 1970s — during which the company operated on very slim margins or, in some cases, no margins at all. The problem was, as Whidden later admitted, "We got way behind in marketing." Paradoxically, these years, tough as they were, also were Whidden's finest in the business. A friend, Ken Cox, president of the New Brunswick Telephone Company, said afterward: "If I had had to give odds at the time, I wouldn't have given him the ghost of a chance."

Struggling to keep the business afloat while striking a balance with family heritage, company tradition, and the need to maintain high quality, Whidden used his own stock as collateral on loans, mortgaged his house and farm, and bought $150,000 in life insurance — payable to the bank. He stubbornly refused to consider selling out to another company.

By the early 1970s, however, it was clear that Ganong's couldn't go on like this much longer. Bank pressures were increasing, the factory was showing its age, new equipment was needed. Whidden put together a core group of his closest company associates to examine the predicament. The group included Bill Cleghorn and Jim Purcell, who were company vice-presidents, and George Ensor's grandson Jack, now the plant's general manager and Whidden's own confidante. Another member was young David Ganong, Whidden's nephew, lately returned to the company after earning a master's degree in business, at the University of Western Ontario.

Meeting in the evenings and on Saturday mornings, the group began the deepest process of soul-searching and introspection the company had ever undertaken. It was, in some ways, a very painful process for Whidden, because no one felt the weight of family heritage and history more than he. He harkened back to that sepia-tinted time when Ganong's sought to fill shops and stores with every candy imaginable. But he also understood that the members of his brain trust were the new navigators of a new age, and he allowed them to proceed.

They recommended drastically reducing the number of Ganong's lines, many of them producing specialty candies in small numbers. When these cuts were made, the company began making money again: by 1989, sales were nearly double what they'd been just a few years before, and profits had risen commensurately. And now Ganong Brothers, whose most palpable symbol of company tradition was the hulking old factory itself, arrived at the threshold of its biggest change ever.

In the mid-1970s, the company began identifying itself simply as "Ganong," a crisp, modern variation on Ganong's."

Ganong

GB

CHOCOLATES
CHOCOLAT

'BUT THEY'RE WORTH IT'

It was the thirty-second TV commercial everybody remembered.

It featured Whidden Ganong, the company's then seventy-seven-year-old chairman, looking handsome and homespun as he describes his family's long history in the candy business. Then he bites into a chocolate from a Delecto box. "They may cost a little more," he says, a shy, half-smile crossing his face, "but they're worth it." No television line was ever uttered with more conviction — or believability.

By this time, in the early 1980s, Whidden had been in the business for well over half a century, and no family member had ever embraced its history and traditions more ardently. All of this came home one memorable night in 1983 when, during a Ganong sales meeting in Florida, he was asked to make a few remarks between dinner and a following dance. He turned the opportunity into a *tour de force*, a memorable recalling of company stories and anecdotes.

The hired orchestra never got a chance to play that night, but Whidden struck some resonant notes of his own. So his nephew, David Ganong, and the company's advertising agency decided to see if the essence of the man and what he stood for could be captured in thirty seconds of television. Aired before Christmas, 1983, the commercial drew a tremendous response. Letters came to the company from all over the country, many with nostalgic reminiscences triggered by the image of this highly believable gentleman from Down Home. Ganongs sold a lot of chocolates, too.

Mr. R.W. Ganong

Commemorative Dinner

On The Occasion of His Ninetieth Bir[...]

October 2, 1996

St. Stephen, New Brunswick

Whidden Ganong's Manifesto

To pay the best wages and salaries possible in keeping with
    a healthy business.
To provide leaders in community activities by encouraging
    our executive staff to take part in them.
To make the best chocolates and candy that can be made.
To provide pleasant working conditions.
To have a reasonably efficient organization without sacrificing
    pleasantness to hard business principles dedicated to
    efficiency alone.
To have an "open door" by management, including top
    management, to all employees at any time.

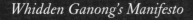

*Left: Limited edition box celebrating
Whidden Ganong's ninetieth birthday,
October 2, 1996.*

GB
**'GANONG's BEST'
CHOCOLATES**

**Available at Bradlees
Gift Wrapped**

95

'IT WOULDN'T BE CHRISTMAS WITHOUT CHICKEN BONES'

Of all the candies made by Ganong Brothers, one is truly unique — Chicken Bones. Consisting of a pink-shaded jacket of hard-boiled sugar and cinnamon covering a generous strand of unsweetened chocolate and shaped, of course, like the bone of a chicken, they were a creation of that brilliant old Ganong candy-maker, Frank Sparhawk, who undoubtedly never imagined they would still be around more than a century later.

Even amid the whirring automation of Ganong's modern factory, Chicken Bones are still made much the way they were at the beginning. Starting with a thick, taffy-like rope of hard candy, the Chicken Bone maker pours into the centre of it an ample amount of "real bitter chocolate." Then, with patience and muscle, the mass is worked until the chocolate is completely covered. And finally, after the mix has been stretched into a thin rope, it is fed into a cutting machine — about the only concession to modernity in the entire process — from which the finished candies emerge, each containing, miraculously, just the right amount of chocolate.

Today's Chicken Bones, each roughly four centimetres long, are half the size they once were. That was in the days when girls in the packing department would stack them vertically one by one in nine-pound tin pails and thirty-pound wooden tubs for shipping, a feat of tireless patience barely imaginable today. Those were also the days when Chicken Bones caught on as a distinctive Maritime Christmas treat, a seasonal habit that persists yet in homes across the region. The passing years have merely added a nostalgic sentiment to the candy's allure. Put into words, it means simply, "It wouldn't be Christmas without Chicken Bones."

Ganong
THE ORIGINAL
Chicken Bones™
Cinnamon candy filled with

THE OLD FACTORY WHISTLE

Like spring birdsong after the long northern winter or the tolling of London's Big Ben in war and peace, certain sounds are inherently reassuring. In St. Stephen, it was the steam whistle atop the old Ganong factory on Milltown Boulevard. For generations, it announced the beginning of every workday — a dependable signal, through good times and bad, that the town's economic mainstay was still there.

"Always make sure that whistle blows," Arthur Ganong decreed long ago. "It shows the success of the business." Just as he adhered to that policy, so, too, did his son Whidden, who succeeded him, and so did his grandson David, when he became company president.

But then came the move, in 1990, to a new Ganong factory on the edge of town. By then, times had changed — no longer was the whistle needed to serve as the town's collective alarm clock, no longer did townspeople have to use its punctual emissions to set their own timepieces.

But a tradition is a tradition. So, when Ganong's moved its operations from downtown St. Stephen to the new location on Chocolate Drive, the whistle went, too. And nowadays, while parts of the factory operate round the clock seven days a week, the old whistle still sounds three times daily, Monday to Friday.

Limited edition box celebrating Arthur D. Ganong, 1990.

Ganong

ARTHUR D. GANONG'S

Especially Assorted

CHOCOLATES · CHOCOLATS

LIMITED EDITION
JUNE 1, 1990

EDITION LIMITEE
1 JUIN, 1990

RE-INVENTING GANONG'S

In June, 1990, Ganong moved to a new factory on the outskirts of St. Stephen. It wasn't easy to vacate the old building, so much a part of life on the town's main street, so bound up with family heritage and tradition. The company had done well over the previous decade and a half, but competition grew tougher than ever as the candy industry continued to consolidate and automate. Ganong recognized that it simply might not survive if it kept operating its century-old factory.

So the company built a new factory. In so doing, it pinned a lot of its hopes for the future on expanding that most traditional part of the business — boxed chocolates. It even added surplus space for "enrobing," or coating, chocolate pieces, in full and eager expectation that the extra space soon would be needed.

The new factory at One Chocolate Drive in St. Stephen.

Unfortunately, the competition had similar designs on the Canadian taste for chocolates. In the early 1990s, Hershey (which acquired Ganong's traditional Maritime rival, Moirs, of Halifax) and Nestlé both mounted aggressive campaigns to sell more boxed chocolates. Another American competitor, Russell Stover, soon joined them, and the combined result was that Ganong's anticipated increase in chocolate sales never materialized.

By 1995, the company was losing money, and when the losses continued in 1996 and 1997, drastic steps had to be taken. Ganong replaced its sales forces in

Revolving pans in the old factory, 1953.

Ontario and western Canada with independent brokers, reduced office staff in St. Stephen by a third, and withdrew from a once-promising joint venture in Southeast Asia. Even office newspaper subscriptions and long-standing company memberships in business organizations were cancelled.

Then, with its survival as an independent, family-owned business now clearly at stake, the company began something even more important. It started another process of critical self-examination, to which it assigned a military-style motivational name — Project Achieve. And by the time that was completed, the company, now under President David Ganong, had not only demonstrated anew its two most abiding characteristics over the decades — resiliency and fidelity to its small-town roots — it had also embarked on nothing short of a dramatic re-invention of itself.

One of the findings of Project Achieve was that one-quarter of the approximately 450 different candies Ganong still made had ceased to be profitable. So the company dropped them. They included almost all of the company's remaining hard candies, the single exception being the celebrated Chicken Bones. Meanwhile, some of the equipment used to make hard candy — the rotating copper machines called "hard pans" — were converted into "soft pans" for polishing jelly beans, for which sales were on the rise.

The company began making money again in 1997. But Project Achieve had revealed something else: "private label" and "contract packing," where Ganong

It only takes a moment to eat a jelly bean, but it takes a whole week to make one. Starting with depositing the clear, unflavoured centres into starch moulds right up to the final stage of polishing and cooling in revolving pans, jelly bean-making hasn't changed much in more than a hundred years. A key step is adding the flavouring and colouring. This takes about twenty-four hours and increases both the size and weight of the 'beans and imparts their distinctive look and taste. Americans are said to eat sixteen billion jelly beans at Easter alone. Canadian consumption is less prodigious, but not so modest that a kids' T-shirt at the Ganong Chocolatier can't proclaim: "I pigged out on Ganong jelly beans."

Above: adding colour to jelly beans.

Left: jelly bean centres are put into a revolving pan for polishing.

Above: visitors view the jelly bean line, circa 1960.

Right: jelly beans are sorted by colour.

makes candy for customers to sell under their own labels and according to their own formulations or recipes, were actually more profitable for the company than some of its own brands, when all costs, including marketing, were taken into account. The inescapable message for the company was: go after more of this kind of business. So Ganong did, in both Canada and the United States.

Although the company was profitable again, it had to grow in order to remain competitive with rivals who were busily acquiring other companies. Ganong couldn't do that because it lacked the financial resources. But perhaps, management figured, it could enlarge itself by playing to its strengths, concentrating on products it was expert at making.

Then the company learned that a world-famous trademark was becoming available in Canada for a product in which it had considerable expertise: fruit snacks. Not a candy in the traditional sense, fruit snacks are a soft and chewy confection made with juice or purée and targeted mainly at children. Ganong

had been making them since the 1980s. Its product was good, but hadn't done especially well on grocery shelves, apparently because nutrition-conscious consumers saw Ganong as a candy company, not as a maker of fruit snacks.

A new trademark could make a difference — especially Sunkist, a name synonymous with citrus fruits and good health. Thomas J. Lipton, the soup people, held the Canadian licence for Sunkist fruit snacks, but wanted to relinquish it.

Sunkist fruit snacks make their way through the assembly line.

Opposite: a computerized weighing machine sends just the right amount of candy into cellophane packages.

To take it over, all Ganong had to do was convince Sunkist that it could do the job. In other words, a little company from the other side of the continent, whom Sunkist had never heard of, had to persuade a billion-dollar California grower co-operative to entrust it with one of the most famous trademarks on the planet!

Undaunted, David Ganong and a company colleague flew to Los Angeles and drove out among the orange groves to the Sunkist headquarters. There, they made a ninety-minute presentation. First, they stressed the business culture of Ganong and the values their company had in common with grower-owned Sunkist. Then, they dealt with their understanding of the fruit snack business and its growth potential in Canada, and how Ganong could achieve that growth. Finally, they answered a few questions.

Sunkist had been seeking a company that was well connected to the grocery business, a large biscuit company, for example. But the Ganong presentation had been well organized, and what struck a particular chord with the Sunkist people

In the early 1930s, at Christmas time, Ganong introduced a special five-pound box of Ganong's Best, . . . a mixture of soft and hard centres. Ganong called it Red Wrap Chocolates because of its bright, festive package. Red Wrap Chocolates have been a Christmas tradition in Atlantic Canada for more than sixty years.

right off the top was the Ganong corporate ethos. They liked the feel of that. The candy company espoused family and community values, and so did farm-based Sunkist — there were a lot of traditional values rooted in its culture, too. The deal was done.

Over the next two years, Ganong acquired the Lipton packaging equipment and organized the Sunkist business, creating a snack called Fruit First and upping its fruit purée content to thirty percent, highest in the industry worldwide. With the same equipment, but different formulations, they also began making fruit snacks for private label customers in the United States and Canada, including most major grocery chains in this country. Eventually, Ganong was turning out ninety percent of Canadian-made fruit snacks, and the item became, for a short time, more voluminous even than chocolates in the company's productive output.

The development of the fruit snack business has been important to Ganong. But Gilbert, the original Ganong chocolate man, need not turn in his grave, since his great-grand-nephew, David still wants the family firm to be known as a chocolate company. How he's managing that is another tale that has unfolded in unexpected places.

In the American Midwest, the green and waving fields of ripening corn that begin just outside of Chicago yield a by-product called glucose, an important ingredient in candy-making. Consequently, Chicago, more famously known for its stockyards and gangsters, long ago also became a confectionery manufacturing centre.

Among the Chicago companies was B.C.I. Confections, founded in 1904 when Emil Brach, with his wife and two sons, opened a small store with a tiny "factory" at the back. The company had subsequently grown into a major of supplier of candies to markets in the United States, Canada, and the rest of the Americas. By the 1990s, however, B.C.I. Confections, like many other American companies, was saddled with an aging factory.

Faced with rising labour and health costs, companies like B.C.I. desperately needed new plants to remain competitive. But, because they were publicly owned, they couldn't build them; the modest returns wouldn't be acceptable to their investors. So, a "purging" was taking place within the industry as companies stopped making candy in their antiquated plants and looked for places where they could outsource its manufacture. Ganong showed up at B.C.I. and won a contract to do the job. Although way off in the Maritime Provinces of Canada, the company had a modern, state-of-the-art factory and an excellent reputation as a candy-maker. For David Ganong and his board, the decision to build in the 1980s, with extra space for making chocolates, suddenly looked a lot better.

Later, Ganong acquired a highly sophisticated chocolate moulding system from the Chicago company. Finally, it purchased B.C.I.'s automatic "cluster" line on which to make those luscious, chocolate-coated, chewy mixtures of caramel and nuts that often bear the name of a certain slow-moving, hard-shelled, terrestrial species.

In 1999, only two years removed from its near-death experience, Ganong was named one of Canada's fifty best-managed private companies. It was a public acknowledgment by the nation's business community that Ganong was on the right track. Still, David knew the company needed to continue to "bulk up" the plant and "thrash" its equipment — in short, to get more production out of the factory.

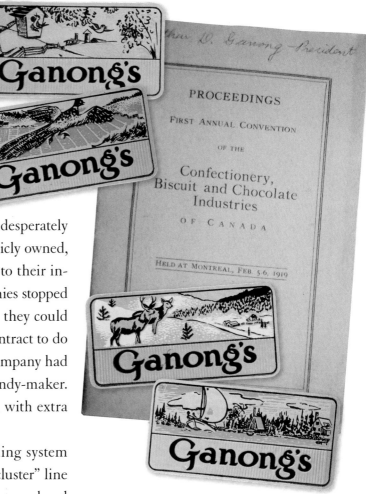

Above: "Four seasons" labels designed by Robert Street, 1963.

Top: Ganong has been part of the national candy industry association since its beginnings in 1919, and three family members have served as its president.

Above: the new assembly line, 2004.

Right: sorting chocolates at the old factory, circa 1940.

Then Ganong learned that the Laura Secord company was looking for someone to make cherry-centred chocolates. Laura Secord had been one of the great Canadian confectionery success stories, a business that grew from a single store in Toronto in 1913 into a national chain. But, by the late twentieth century, an American firm named Archibald owned it, and Archibald had consolidated several candy companies into another of those old Chicago factories. And that was the problem: the factory was old, Archibald was losing money.

Shortly after Ganong opened discussions with it, Archibald filed for U.S. Chapter 11 bankruptcy protection. This, understandably, cast a chill over the talks, but time passed, Archibald emerged from under its cloud, and discussions resumed. Then, one day in 2003, as Laura Secord technicians were about to visit St. Stephen, Archibald called David Ganong to ask how many other Laura Secord pieces his company might also be able to make.

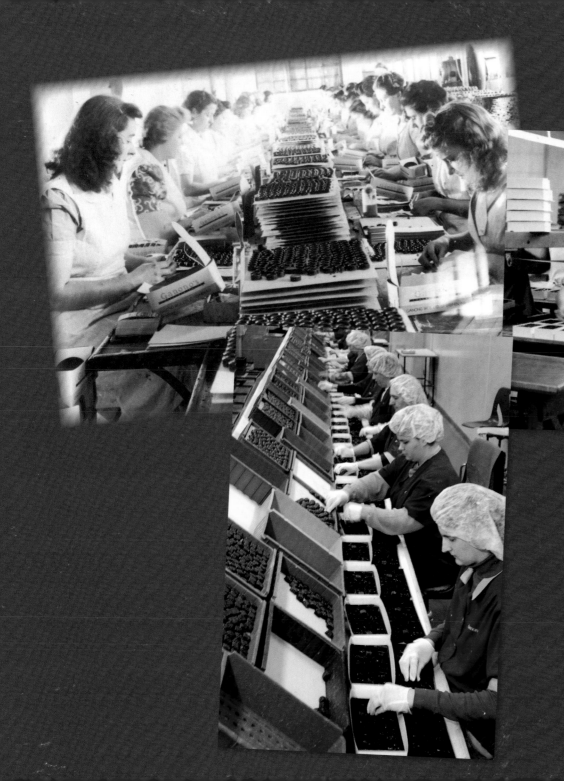

*Wrapping Pepts bar, 1940 (top left),
packing chocolates at the old factory,
1970 (above), and on the current line
in the new plant, 2004 (right).
The methods and attire have
evolved over time.*

1970s photo, NB Power

109

THE GLOBE AND MAIL
THURSDAY, SEPTEMBER 11, 2003

Race heats up to scoop venerable Laura Secord

Real estate firm that owns Cotton Ginny said among bidders

BY MARINA STRAUSS
RETAILING REPORTER

The race to scoop up the venerable chocolatier **Laura Secord** has heated up among the few parties still in the running, including a real estate firm that acquired Cotton Ginny this year, industry sources say.

As well, a group consisting of Hallmark Canada, M & M Meat Shops of Kitchener, Ont., and an unnamed investor is also considering bidding for the chain of 174 stores, sources said yesterday.

Continental Saxon Group, a real estate investment firm that bought the bankrupt clothier Cotton Ginny earlier this year, has bid an amount believed to be $20-million or more for Laura Secord, sources said.

Industry insiders expect Laura Secord could fetch between $20-million and $25-million.

Observers said that dozens of companies and parties expressed interest in swallowing Laura Secord, which was put on the block last April by parent Archibald Candy Corp. of Chicago.

Some questioned the potential for operational synergies between Continental Saxon's Cotton Ginny chain and Laura Secord, although they both operate in malls across the country.

"Laura Secord is a great brand name," said retail consultant John Williams of J.C. Williams Group Ltd. "It's a Canadian institution."

Pace declined to comment.

Laura Secord has suffered from neglect by Archibald Candy, which emerged from bankruptcy protection recently, industry insiders agree. The chain is in dire need of a fresh focus and more investment,

Shoppers browse at a Laura Secord store in the Toronto-Dominion Centre in Toronto. The chain, with annual sales of about $76-million, has faced mounting competition.

they said.

Roger Baranowski, president of Hallmark, said his company has been talking with Laura Secord's advisers but has not put in a bid. "It's not dead," he said, adding that Hallmark's parent in Kansas City, Mo., will have the final say.

The greeting card company already has a joint venture with Laura Secord, operating 18 combination outlets in Canada.

Michael Levy, a partner at Paragon Capital Partners LLC in New York, the investment banker for Archibald, would not comment on possible suitors, although he confirmed there had been a lot of interest in Laura Secord.

Mr. Levy said he expects the sale process to be completed by the end of November.

"There are multiple parties exploring multiple transactions," he said, describing the number as "more than a couple and fewer than a handful."

The investment banker invited a small number of parties to conduct due diligence on a purchase, and they are now submitting "firm proposals."

Meanwhile, the coffee and muffin chain Treats also submitted an offer for Laura Secord, although it is not currently in the running, said Dan Amadori, an adviser to Treats.

He said the franchised Treats would make a good fit with the chocolatier and would run it as a franchised operation. The Treats offer was a complex one that was

Deal on Laura Secord expected soon

Price for candy maker could reach $25 million, sources say
Purchase would bring chocolate production back to Canada

DANA FLAVELLE
BUSINESS REPORTER

A major financier with significant retail experience is behind controversial Montreal businessman Gaetan Frigon's bid for Laura Secord, Canada's best-known premium chocolate-candy maker, sources close to the deal say.

Laura Secord's owner, the Archibald Candy Corp. of Chicago, is expected to announce by Nov. 1 that it has reached an agreement with a buyer for the 174-store chain, sources also said.

Frigon, who was embroiled in a Quebec political scandal earlier this year, was unavailable for comment yesterday. However, he is considered the front-runner in the competition to buy the profitable but neglected business.

The deal is expected to fetch between $20 million and $25 million for Archibald Candy and

would involve repatriating production of the chocolates, sources said.

The chocolates are currently produced in Chicago, headquarters of Archibald Candy, which put Laura Secord up for sale last April, less than four years after buying the company from Swiss-owned Nestlé Canada Inc.

Production would move to the New Brunswick-based chocolatier Ganong Bros. Ltd., sources said.

David Ganong, president of the privately held family business, confirmed his company first approached Archibald Candy two years ago with the idea of supplying its needs.

"We would be interested in doing that for whoever buys the company," he added.

Ganong estimates Laura Secord's production would create

40 to 50 new jobs at its St. Stephen, N.B., plant. The oldest and second largest maker of boxed chocolates in Canada currently employs 260 people, he said.

The deal is seen as good for the Laura Secord brand, which had been neglected after Archibald Candy, which also owns two leading U.S. chocolate companies, ran into financial difficulty.

➤ Please see **Sweet**, E11

Ganong's wraps up sweet deal

BY ANDREW PHILIPS
Telegraph-Journal

MANUFACTURING: St. Stephen candymakers to produce treats for Laura Secord

Now, that's a sweet deal. Ganong Bros. Ltd. has signed a major agreement to begin producing candy for Laura Secord chocolate stores, a move that will add about 40 jobs at the company's St. Stephen manufacturing plant, which currently employs 290.

"It means a lot to us," Greg Fash, Ganong's vice-president of strategic marketing, said Monday. "It's substantial, a five-year supply agreement."

Neither side would reveal how much the deal is worth, but Mr. Fash said it will lead to a "substantial increase in our chocolate production."

Mr. Fash said he's confident Laura Secord will continue to

prosper, despite recent overtures by its Chicago-based parent company, Archibald Candy Corp., that it wanted to sell the chain.

"We're looking to a long future," he said, noting the agreement is renewable and should also help Ganong attract more business from other parties. "It's a platform for future growth."

Mr. Fash, who pointed out Ganong will faithfully produce the chocolates using Laura Secord's original formulas and recipes, said some production has already started with the remainder scheduled to be

phased in over the next six to 12 months.

Last week, Archibald sold its U.S. business to a fast-growing chocolate manufacturer with operations on both sides of the border. The buyer of its two U.S. brands, Fannie May and Fanny Farmer, was Alpine Confections Inc., a Salt Lake City, Utah, specialist in boxed chocolates.

But that sale raised questions about who would supply the Laura Secord chain, which will soon lose its source of supply when Archibald shutters its Chicago plant.

Archibald Candy Corp.

spokesman Ron Bottrell said Ganong was a good fit because it's a Canadian company with a solid reputation and a proven track record.

While Mr. Bottrell said Laura Secord stores will continue to operate, he wouldn't comment on whether a potential sale is still in the offing.

"The key thing is that their supplier previously had been the Archibald manufacturing plant in Chicago, which is in the process of being closed," he said. "I can only tell you that Laura Secord continues to operate as a separate entity for the foreseeable future."

Laura Secord, named after the War of 1812 heroine, was founded in 1913 and acquired by Archibald in 1999. It has 165 outlets in Canada.

Andrew Philips/Telegraph-Journal
New Brunswick consumers purchasing sweets at Laura Secord outlets like this one in Dieppe's Champlain Place will soon be helping to support St. Stephen's economy.

It sounded good, but this news, too, was soon clouded by information that Archibald was getting ready to seek bankruptcy protection again and was trying to sell the candy companies clustered under its Chicago roof. As many as half a dozen suitors showed interest in Laura Secord; and Ganong, staying the course, talked to them all. Finally, a Montreal-based financial house was the apparent winner. In the ensuing months, David Ganong worked hard at brokering a deal among the financial house, Archibald, and his own company. He also invested, under financial protections, about two million dollars in new equipment that would be needed to make the Laura Secord candies.

By November, 2003, the deal appeared set, and David, exhausted after the long negotiations and repeated travel from St. Stephen to Montreal and Chicago, made plans for a Mexican vacation. He and his wife Diane were headed for the airport in Saint John when, making a final check with his office, he learned that the owner of Archibald, David Markus, was desperately trying to reach him. The deal was off — Archibald had, at the last minute, decided the conditions imposed by the financial house were too onerous.

In the end, the Montreal firm did not buy Laura Secord. Another investment house, Gordon Brothers Group LLC of Boston, did, and Ganong finally got its long-sought contract. Soon, the company was making a major part of Laura Secord chocolates and packing most of its assortments. And chocolates had once again become Ganong's biggest product.

In the decade that began with the financial crisis of the mid-1990s, the Ganong company had essentially re-invented itself, developing an expertise in new products, like fruit snacks, and greatly enlarging the private label and contract packing side of the business. All the while, it had also kept up its own brands and candies — those that had earned the company its reputation in the first place.

THE WORLD'S OLDEST CANDY MACHINE?

Sugar was the commodity that spread candy's popularity throughout the world — but it was nineteenth-century manufacturing machinery that made it available to the masses. Remarkably, one of those vintage machines is still at work in the Ganong factory.

The machine came out of the Industrial Revolution. Gilbert Ganong brought it from Europe in 1889, when he was building a new factory. Installed on the third floor, it transformed production of lozenges from a hand operation into an automated one that produced thousands of pounds daily. In fact, the machine worked so well that Gilbert subsequently bought a second one, and thereafter lozenges, which include mints, cough drops, wafers, and multi-coloured heart-shaped pieces, poured out in massive quantities.

Then an awful thing happened. The fire of 1903 struck, and the two lozenge machines crashed through to the ground. They were almost hopelessly damaged. But Gilbert had some clever mechanics in his employ, and they set to work to see what they could salvage from the twisted wreckage. In the end, they managed to find enough pieces to make one machine — the one that is still running today, well over a century later. It may be the oldest working candy machine in the world.

In a factory room where a small wall plaque honours the memory of Chris Laubman, the original Ganong lozenge-maker, the rumbling old machine cranks out 800,000 individual white, pink, and green mints in a ten-hour shift. With four shifts a week, the potential weekly output is more than three million mints. As for the numbers the machine has turned out over the years, decades, century . . . well . . . the mind merely boggles.

Above: The lozenge machine, purchased in 1889, and shown here in 1943, is still running today.

DAVID GANONG: GIRDING FOR THE CHALLENGE

Even as a child, David Ganong naturally was aware that his father Philip worked at the candy factory, and one of his more impish memories is of tossing apples from a nearby orchard into the factory through an open window, then racing inside to dip them in caramel before throwing them back outside. Later, as a student, he learned through direct experience how much muscle it took to unload a boxcar of sugar, and what it felt like to be covered with starch.

Still, when he graduated from the University of New Brunswick, David felt no particular compulsion to choose the family business as a career, and he worked briefly for DuPont Canada, in Montreal, before joining Ganong Brothers as Whidden's assistant in 1966. Three years later, he left to earn a master's degree in business at the University of Western Ontario, taking as many sales and marketing courses as he could find. (His uncle Whidden, at sixty-four, also enrolled in a three-week course at Western in order to have some grasp of the modern concepts his nephew might bring back to the company.)

David signed on permanently with Ganong in the spring of 1970. Seven years later, he succeeded Whidden as company president. In the interim, he played an important role, along with other company executives, in engineering Ganong's return to profitability in the middle of the 1970s. An unquestioned pragmatist, he found it easier to cut traditional candy lines than did Whidden. And when the company faced the crisis of the mid-1990s, that experience served him well.

David Ganong in 1977, the year he became president.

David Ganong with daughter
Bryana, 2003

LOOKING TOWARD THE FUTURE

In 2006, David Ganong marked his thirtieth year as president of Ganong Brothers. During that period, he has become one of Canada's outstanding business executives, the recipient of numerous national awards. Besides guiding his own company, he has served on the boards of Air Canada and Mutual Life of Canada. A few years after joining the latter's board, he became its chair, just in time to preside over the firm's complicated transition from a mutual, or policy-holder-owned, company to one owned by stockholders, and renamed Clarica. It was a heavy load, but he felt the exposure to new people and the ways of the wider business world made it worthwhile for his own company, too. It was, he said, "quite an experience for a little guy from Down Home."

David has never been short on ambition, something his grandfather Arthur perceived long ago while watching him zealously at play. In his sixties, he remains highly energized and involved, and could still be many years away from retirement. (His grandfather was racing younger employees up the steps of the old factory at 83; his uncle, Whidden, gave up the company presidency at 71 but remained on the board for many more years.) But what will happen when David does finally yield the reins? It should be no surprise that, as someone known for attention to detail, he has already done a lot of planning for that.

The Ganong chocolatier is part of the refurbished old factory, as is the Chocolate Museum.

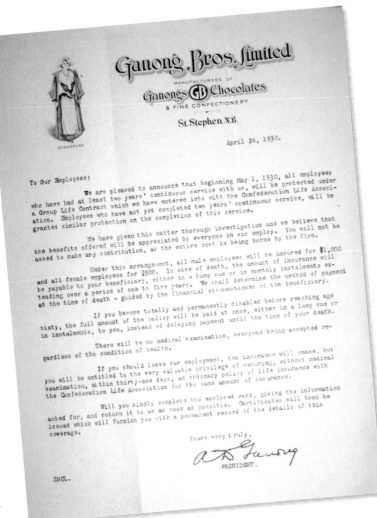

Above: letter to employees from A.D. Ganong announcing insurance coverage for all with more than two years' service with the company.

He and Diane have three children, Bryana, Aaron, and Nicholas, and traditionalists will be pleased to know that two of them are in the family business. Bryana is a member of the firm's management, and coordinates the private label and contract packing facet of the business; Nicholas is a production supervisor.

However the succession unfolds, the company presidency will not automatically devolve to one of the young Ganongs. He or she will have to earn it "in the eyes of somebody other than me," said their father. The company's board of directors and three overseers of a family trust will make that determination.

David has been similarly prudent in establishing the roadmap to future ownership of the company. An abiding concern is Ganong's importance to St. Stephen. "From my APEC days," he said of his term as chairman of the Atlantic Provinces Economic Council for 1984-1985, "I developed a strong view that, when ownership leaves the region, the jobs aren't far behind."

Currently, ninety-three percent of Ganong shares are safely in David's hands, bought by him over a long period that ended only in 2004. He has never planned

Above: Employees' time log from November 1911.

Left: Employees mark Ganong's 125th anniversary, 1998.

St. Stephen's candy-making tradition doesn't reside only in the Ganong family. Ganong currently employs 310 people in the town of five thousand, several of whom represent the second, third, and even fourth generations of their families to work for the candy company.

on disposing of them in a conventional way, by selling them to the highest bidder. Instead, should one of the Ganong children not become company president, he has mandated the family trust to pursue other options designed to keep the ownership local. One is to sell the shares, at less than the market price, to company employees, with everybody from the chief executive officer to the cleaning crew eligible to buy. If that can't be worked out, the shares should at least be sold to a New Brunswick purchaser. And only if that fails would the shares be put on the open market. It is "kind of a crazy philosophy for a businessman," David admitted, "but, anyway, that's what I've done." His innate pragmatism notwithstanding, David Ganong is, in the final analysis, every bit as committed to tradition and community as were his ancestral predecessors.

"I learned tremendous lessons from my uncle," Ganong says. "The most important had to do with treating our employees fairly. That was always a priority with him, as it had been for his father, Arthur. Secondly, he was a maniac when it came to quality. Everything, no matter what the pressures were, had to be the very best. When it wasn't, he could be very difficult for various managers — including me — to deal with. Finally, his commitment to the local community was unparalleled. He really believed he owed a debt to society, and he demonstrated that in a dozen different ways."

— David Ganong in
"Atlantic Canada First,"
Alec Bruce, 2006.

BRYANA, A NEW FACE FOR GANONG

Young and knowledgeable about chocolate, David and Diane Ganong's daughter Bryana seems a natural to be a public spokesperson for the family business. She even had the good fortune to be born into Canada's premier chocolate family on Valentine's Day.

But when first approached with the idea and given an elaborate presentation on how it could be done, Bryana was less than enthusiastic. She was, after all, a very private person who couldn't imagine how she could carry it off: "It was a big stretch for me."

Finally agreeing, she did well at product launches, promotional events, and in media interviews. The most agonizing experience turned out to be filming a thirty-second Christmas TV commercial, done in winter clothing, during two sixteen-hour sweltering summer days in southern Ontario.

The side of the business she prefers is working with colleagues in the factory. After more than a decade there, she's learned a lot about chocolate — how it's made, the technology involved, what it takes to make a successful box of chocolates. When the question about her future with the company comes up, as it inevitably does, she gives a prompt and essentially non-committal answer: "At this point in my life, I can't imagine working anywhere else."

The annual Chocolate Festival parade *(left)*. St. Croix Courier

Street scene in St. Stephen, New Brunswick, circa 1906 *(above)*. Provincial Archives of New Brunswick, P11-105

DOWN HOME COMPANY, NATIONAL INSTITUTION

There was a time when, as you strolled along St. Stephen's main street, you could tell what candies they were making in the candy factory just by sniffing the air. Those sensuous times may be gone, but there's still plenty of evidence of the Ganong presence in the town.

A large sign in a traffic circle at a highway intersection proclaims this as "Canada's Chocolate Town." Nearby is the new company factory, located on Chocolate Drive, no less. From here, the sound of the factory whistle still wafts over the town. On the main street, there's a community-run Chocolate Museum and the Ganong Chocolatier store, both housed in the old factory, now refurbished as Ganong Place and still the soul of the downtown. And there's an annual chocolate festival, an Eleanor Deacon Ganong Rose Garden, a St. Stephen Chocolate Park, and, a few kilometres down the St. Croix River, the Ganong Nature & Marine Park.

These are the contemporary manifestations of a symbiotic relationship that has existed between the Ganongs and the town since the days when James Ganong was a community activist and Gilbert supported a new St. Stephen band with a crisp ten-dollar bill and gave local fishermen a hundred dollars for a trip to Europe to learn fish-curing methods. The community involvement of the company and family has been nothing if not comprehensive. Once, in an undepend-

Chef carving chocolate to mark the annual Run for the Cure at Union Station, Toronto, 2003.

able winter, Ganong's hooked the town's outdoor rink to the factory refrigeration system, and Whidden Ganong, who also happened to be mayor at the time, took turns with his brother Philip at supervising the skating.

The Ganongs have exercised a leadership role for so long that it now seems bred in the bone. Three generations have provided mayors for the town, in the persons of James, Arthur, and Whidden; two Ganongs, Gilbert and Arthur, were Members of Parliament; and all of the company presidents, including David, have been recognized regional and national business leaders.

As one might expect, both the company and the family have long supported all manner of public projects and activities. Beneficiaries today range from local sports teams to university scholarship winners, from a local transition house to the Muriel McQueen Institute for Family Violence in Fredericton. In 2005, the company created the Ganong Chocolate Scholarship for St. Stephen High School graduates at the University of New Brunswick, and David and Diane Ganong added scholarship for students learning French as a second language, as well as funds for the processing of Ganong papers at the university's Harriet Irving Library.

Nationally, the company began, in 2003, a relationship with the Canadian Breast Cancer Foundation, becoming a major sponsor of the Canadian Imperial Bank of Commerce Run for the Cure, which each autumn raises millions of medical research dollars. The link between the breast cancer campaign's pink ribbon symbol and the pink of Ganong Chicken Bones was a natural one. The company gives a specially designed pink "memory box" of chocolates to each of the thousands of volunteers who help organize the run, and in 2005 it also produced fifty thousand packages of pink jelly beans for sale at C.I.B.C. branches across the country as a further fund-raising venture. The company benefits, too, by introducing a lot of new people to its candies, highly important to a small company with limited advertising dollars competing in a fragmented media universe.

As a determinedly Maritime company whose history and long traditions have given it a national cachet, Ganong is the sort of institution you want to root for. Dr. Margaret Conrad, holder of the Canada Research Chair in Atlantic Studies at U.N.B., notes that it is one of the few surviving companies coming out of the National Policy — longevity alone would be reason enough for championing it. As well, homegrown success stories like that of Ganong sometimes seem "the only things keeping Maritimers from economic despair." Such companies "give us importance in the business world," she says, and they also support a host of local, regional ,and national organizations through their financial generosity and the volunteer work of their owners and employees.

Above: Eleanor and Whidden Ganong on the verandah of their cottage at Todd's Point.

Top: Ganong Nature & Marine Park at Todd's Point, near St. Stephen.

St. Croix Estuary Project.

And that of their wives. Maria Ganong, Gilbert's wife, left a will that greatly benefited the immediate community (their former residence, Lonicera Hall, now a seniors' home, is an example), while Arthur's wife Berla, a voracious reader, regularly distributed a litter of newspaper clippings round the house that broadened her children's outlooks, fueled family discussions, and made her an influential leader among the ladies of the community who regularly gathered at her home. And Whidden's wife Eleanor supplied steady companionship and a great shared interest in her husband's enthusiasms, especially market gardening at their cherished summer place at Todd's Point, now the site of the Ganong Nature & Marine Park.

Diane Ganong, from the nearby rural community of Waweig, where she went to a one-room school, grew up in a time when society was redefining the roles of women. She and David met when both were home for Christmas, 1968 — she from nurses' training at Montreal's Royal Victoria Hospital, he from his master's degree studies at the University of Western Ontario. They married four years later.

In 1979, Diane was recruited to sell Christmas cards for UNICEF, the United Nations Children's Fund, and from there she went on to join the local organization in St. Stephen, then became a representative on UNICEF's provincial board, and finally its chair. In the late 1980s, on a UNICEF-sponsored study trip to Indonesia, she saw how effectively money from Canada was being used, and her conversion to the cause was complete. By 1994, she was president of UNICEF Canada.

Traveling with her husband to countries such as Thailand, Argentina, and Brazil, Diane took the opportunity to visit places where she saw "quite astounding" levels of poverty. In Cambodia, she watched the clearing of deadly landmines, eerily toy-like in appearance and some buried close to schools. Eventually, she began studies in international development at McGill University, graduating in 2001, and she has since continued to raise funds for UNICEF while also working with several other organizations. She has also been, since 1998, the first Ganong wife to serve on the company board.

Like Diane's, many of David Ganong's outside activities are born of a natural interest and inclination. The responsibilities he feels as a Ganong belong in a category by themselves. There was, for example, the matter of the old factory, so long a landmark

Ganong's Chocolates GB An Assortment of Family Favorites SYLVAN PACKAGE NET WEIGHT 1 LB.

in downtown St. Stephen. Putting together a new multi-use concept for the building, which seemed the best way of saving it, was anything but simple in the small town. According to the developer who ultimately did the restoration, it was primarily David's tenacity that "kept the project alive." He involved several others, including then-Premier of New Brunswick Frank McKenna, and whenever they met, Ganong always made sure chocolates were handy to nibble on. Later, during a brief term as Canadian ambassador to the United States, McKenna himself kept an ample supply of Ganong chocolates to serve at the embassy in Washington.

The restoration of the old factory cost eight million dollars, some of which came from the Atlantic Canada Opportunities Agency. The restoration contractor

The old factory was restored to house a chocolatier, The Chocolate Museum, and a number of office and residential units.

who did the job, Dick Carpenter of Moncton, remembered how, when they started job, the fragrance of candy still permeated the wood. But even more appealing were the building's high ceilings and numerous windows, which, said Carpenter, enabled him to do interesting things. And today it is a fine, sensible restoration, with apartments, a restaurant, a credit union, and government and other offices, in addition to The Chocolate Museum and the Chocolatier store. The heritage of Ganong Place is acknowledged in various ways, with exposed brick walls and lots of vintage photographs, and with the factory's former walk-in vault serving as the Chocolatier's modern cold room for keeping chocolates fresh.

Another symbol from bygone days is the old factory weather vane on the roof, which showed generations of passers-by the direction of the sweetened breezes. Then, one day about two years after the restoration was finished, it suddenly fetched up and stopped turning. Only one person knew how it could be fixed — Whidden Ganong, who remembered that its gears had been scalped from a 1929 Model 'T' Ford. So, another set of gears was found, the weather vane was repaired, and St. Stephen knew again which way the wind was blowing.

Businesses like Ganong are more than faces in the corporate crowd. They have a distinctive social-cultural impact and an iconic value that transcend mere economics. In a very real sense, they are part of *us*, an emblem and an exemplar for a town, a region, a whole country. Prime Minister Lester Pearson, receiving a promise of some Texas pralines from U.S. President Lyndon Johnson in 1967, replied: "I'll send you some Ganong mints." Every Christmas, New Brunswickers dispatch gifts of Chicken Bones, more durable than fiddleheads and equally distinctive, to friends, acquaintances, and ex-pats all over

the world. Ganong memorabilia, everything from lithographed tin candy pails to sets of Big Chief collector cards, some selling for hundreds of dollars, regularly show up on eBay.

So, the responsibility that David Ganong bears as his company's president has a whole other dimension to that of the average corporate executive, and it's one that sometimes has to be defended, even within the walls of his own boardroom. Not long ago, he was asked just how far he might be willing to go to keep the company attached to its small-town St. Stephen roots. David's reply was straightforward and familiar: "As long as we can continue to operate economically in St. Stephen," he said, "the goal is to keep it here."

A DELECTO TALE

Early in the last century, having satisfied himself that boxed chocolates were here to stay, Gilbert Ganong — perhaps in collaboration with his nephew Arthur and one or more of their inspired candy-makers — decided to package the company's premium chocolates under a special name. They called the new box Delecto, giving the word "delectable" a slightly cosmopolitan twist for the increasingly effervescent times.

Today Delecto is Ganong's oldest brand name, older even than Chicken Bones and the Pal-o-Mine bar. It is also the most popular box of assorted chocolates in Canada.

Naturally, there have been many manifestations of the Delecto box during the brand's long life. Even when the horse-and-coach theme ruled the box's decorative style, there were subtle changes. Finally, in 1970, the company broke with tradition in favour of a more modern look. The box and its contents have continued to evolve, so that, in 2006, Ganong introduced both a new package and a new line of Delecto chocolates. It's the broadest chocolate assortment the company has ever had, and it's made possible, interestingly enough, by a sweet synergy of old and new — Ganong's traditional favourites as well as new pieces made on machines the company got for its contract packing business.

ST. STEPHEN'S CHOCOLATE FESTIVAL

As a hometown boy, Duncan McGeachy felt for a long time that St. Stephen hadn't taken full advantage of its chocolate heritage. So, one day in the early 1980s, "I went in and had a talk with David [Ganong]. I asked him, 'How would you feel if we started a chocolate festival?' Then we got a group together, and it took off quite well."

So it did. Now more than two decades old, Chocolate Fest has a line-up of chocolate-related events: contests in pudding eating, hand-dipping, and decorating; the selection of a Chocolate Lover of the Year; and meals that feature chocolate, including a spectacular brunch at nearby St. Andrews' famed resort hotel, the Algonquin. There's a festival mascot, Chocolate Mousse, and, for the only time during the year, the Ganong factory is open for public tours.

The unique festival, held each year in the first week of August, attracts not only visitors to St. Stephen but also a fair amount of media attention — McGeachy recalls receiving telephone calls from as far away as Australia. "I've always felt that what's good for Ganong is good for the town," he says.

Photos courtesy *St. Croix Courier*

INDEX